Better Homes and Gardens®

A Cross-Stitch
CHRISTMAS®

Handmade Heirlooms

Elizabeth M. Bird

June 2002

Better Homes and Gardens® Creative Collection™
Des Moines, Iowa

Better Homes and Gardens.

A Cross-Stitch
CHRISTMAS®

Creative Director Patricia Church Podlasek
Executive Editor Mary Heaton
Contributing Editor Susan M. Banker
Associate Art Director Greg Sellers
Contributing Graphic Designer Stacey Heston

Editorial Project Coordinator Lauri Duvall
Editorial Assistant Cathy Celsi
Contributing Writers Laura Collins, Rhonda Matus
Contributing Copy Editors Colleen Johnson, Gail Kimel,
Jennifer Phelps, Margaret Smith
Contributing Illustrator Chris Neubauer Graphics

Group Publisher Maureen Ruth
Consumer Product Marketing Director Ben Jones
Consumer Product Marketing Manager Karrie Nelson
Business Manager Jie Lin
Production Director Douglas M. Johnston
Production Managers Pam Kvitne, Marjorie J. Schenkelberg

Vice President and Publishing Director
William R. Reed

Chairman and CEO
William T. Kerr
Chairman of the Executive Committee
E.T. Meredith III

Meredith Publishing Group

Publishing Group President Stephen M. Lacy
Magazine Group President Jerry Kaplan
Group Sales Michael Brownstein
Creative Services Ellen de Lathouder
Manufacturing Bruce Heston
Consumer Marketing Karla Jeffries
Finance and Administration Max Runciman

 Our Mark of Excellence seal assures you
that every project in this book has been
constructed and checked under the direction of
the cross-stitch experts at *Better Homes and
Gardens® Creative Collection™.*

Member
HiA
HOBBY INDUSTRY
ASSOCIATION

Crafts.
Discover life's little
pleasures.

For book editorial questions, write
Better Homes and Gardens® A Cross-Stitch Christmas
1716 Locust St.–GA 201,
Des Moines, IA 50309-3023;
phone 515/284-3623; fax 515/284-3115.
For additional copies or billing questions,
call 800/322-0691.

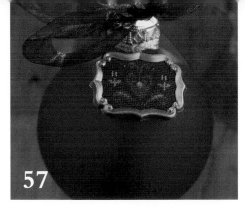

57

Contents

A Cross-Stitch CHRISTMAS.

20

6

For cross-stitchers, the Christmas season

brings a sense of childhood merriment. This wondrous time of year gives us stitchers the joyful opportunity to create floss-and-fabric works of art. We proudly display our stitched pieces as we trim our holiday homes. We stitch special greetings to send "Merry Christmas" wishes afar. And we live for the moments when we can present stitched surprises to those who are dear to our hearts. Yes, Christmas is a magical time that prompts a flourish of creativity.

Whether you are about to start your first cross-stitched treasure or you already have a repertoire of projects to your credit, we hope you'll find hours of enjoyment in this book. To ensure your success, each holiday project is accompanied by an easy-to-read color chart and a key as well as step-by-step instructions. And if you are new to the technique, the Cross-Stitch Basics on *pages 122–125* will provide everything you'll need to know from the first merry stitch to the last. So, as you prepare to celebrate the wonder of Christmas in stitches, we hope you'll find here all the inspiration you'll need to create exquisite

Handmade Heirlooms.

Christmas Long Ago

Bring sentiment to the holidays
through inspirational stitchery.

Although more than two thousand

years have passed since that very

first Christmas, the essence of the

event remains dear to our hearts.

Now as then we glorify the birth of

the Christ Child, gathering our loved

ones around us in celebration. This

wondrous cross-stitch collection

reflects the holiday's history and

beloved traditions developed through the years. Choose an

old-world St. Nick, an extraordinarily beautiful nativity, a

serene church, or any of the other scenes captured on fabric.

Each of these remembrances will make a lasting impression

as you celebrate the season year after year.

In a stable long ago, Mary and Joseph celebrated the first Christmas. In this exquisite rendition, the story of the Holy Family is depicted in textured stitches. A joy to sew and a delight for the soul, the finished piece expresses reverence for the miracle of the season.

Project instructions begin on page 24. Design: Diana Thomas.

Throughout Advent, families and friends gather for worship, music, and festive holiday preparations. This architectural representation of a church, worked in cross-stitches and delicate white-on-white hardanger, welcomes Christmas as a vision seen through a cutwork window.

Project instructions begin on page 16. Design: Patricia Andrle.

What is it about a winter's eve that causes us to pause? For just a moment, the stars seem brighter, the air we breathe seems fresher, and everything stands still. This composition calls to mind the hushed beauty and sense of wonder of a snowy night.

Project instructions begin on page 14. Design: BrightNeedle.

The magic of Santa Claus is steeped in old-world tradition. Adapted from a vintage

watercolor, Father Christmas bears nature's treasures. Although we may be more familiar with a

plump Santa, this St. Nicholas more closely resembles the original lanky gift-giver.

Project instructions begin on page 21. Design: Barbara Anderson.

In anticipation of the day, three bundled babies are gleeful to greet your guests. This traditional scene of childhood merriment will bring smiles to all who see it. Bedecked with mistletoe and antique-style lettering, the stitchery is sure to become a holiday favorite.

Project instructions begin on page 27. Design: Carol Emmer.

Santa's profile against a starry night makes a striking central design on this holiday
ornament. Created of mostly whole stitches, this project provides the perfect opportunity to
teach cross-stitching to new needlework artists, or you can make several of these Santas as gifts.

Project instructions begin on page 26. Design: Sharon Mann.

Peace on Earth Banner

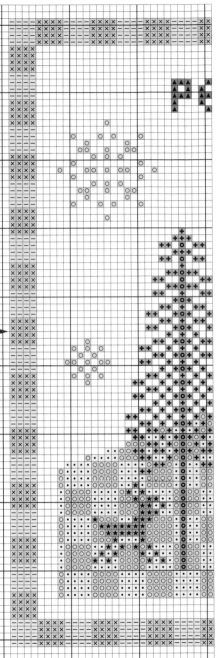

Peace on Earth Banner

Supplies

- 14×12" piece of R&R Reproductions 32-count Liberty Gathering Grey linen
- Kreinik Milkpaint and Silk Mori floss
- Needlepoint Silks floss
- ⅓ yard green-print cotton fabric
- ⅛ yard rust-print cotton fabric
- 14×12" rectangle lightweight quilt batting
- Matching sewing thread

Stitches

Center and stitch the chart on the linen. Use two plies of floss to work the cross-stitches over two threads of the fabric unless otherwise specified. Press the stitched piece from the back.

Assembly

Centering the design, trim stitched piece to a 9×7" rectangle. From the rust-print fabric, cut two 1×7" side border strips and two 1×10" top and bottom border strips. All measurements include a ¼" seam allowance unless otherwise specified.

With right sides together, sew the 1×7" border strips to the left and right edges of the stitched piece. Press seam allowances toward the border. Sew the 1×10" border strips to the top and bottom edges of the stitched piece.

From the green-print fabric, cut a 14×12" backing, two 1¾×8" side sashing strips, two 1¾×12½" top and bottom sashing strips, four 3×5½" hanging tabs, and enough 1½"-wide bias strips to make a continuous length of 48" for the binding.

Sew the 1¾×8" green sashing strips to left and right edges of rust border. Press seam allowances toward sashing strips. Sew the 1¾×12½" green sashing strips to the top and bottom edges of the rust border.

Place the 14×12" back, wrong side up, on a smooth surface. Center and smooth the quilt batting on top. Center the front on the batting and pin-baste all layers together. Machine-stitch in the ditch where the outer edges of the stitched piece meet the rust border. Baste ¼" from the outer edges of the front. Trim the back and batting even with the front.

For each hanging tab, fold a 3×5½" strip in half lengthwise with right sides together; sew the long edges together. Turn the strip right side out. Press, centering the seam down the center back of the strip. Bring the raw edges of the strip together to form a tab. Position the tabs at the top back of the banner, raw edges even with raw edges of banner, placing tabs ¾" from each

top corner and 1½" from each corner tab. Sew across each tab ¼" from the raw edges.

Sew the short ends of the 1½"-wide bias binding strips together for a continuous length and press the binding strip in half lengthwise. Pin the binding to the front of the banner, raw edges even. Using a ¼" seam allowance, sew through all layers, mitering the corners. Turn the binding over the edge of the banner to the back. Hand-sew the binding to the back, covering any machine stitching.

Peace On Earth Banner Key

CROSS-STITCH (2X)

ANCHOR		DMC
235	◰	169 Pewter
855	◆	370 Pecan
233	▤	451 Dark shell gray
232	∧	452 Medium shell gray
862	✚	520 Olive drab
393	◨	640 Dark beige-gray
392	✛	642 Medium beige-gray
885	❘	677 Old gold
390	•	822 Pale beige-gray
8581	✕	3022 Medium brown-gray
040	▬	3023 Light brown-gray
903	★	3032 Medium mocha
267	▦	3362 Loden
899	▽	3782 Light mocha

CROSS-STITCH (2X)

ANCHOR		DMC
1088	◉	3790 Deep beige-gray
313	☆	3854 Autumn gold
897	▲	3857 Rosewood

CROSS-STITCH (1X)

ANCHOR		DMC
313	✷	3854 Autumn gold
	○	992 Kreinik Needlepoint Silk Off-white
	⊕	804 Kreinik Milkpaint Medium cobblestone
	⟋	813 Kreinik Milkpaint Medium flint

Stitch count: 92 high x 128 wide
Finished design size:
32-count fabric – 5¾ x 8 inches

Christmas Church

The charts, keys, and diagrams are on pages 17–20.

Christmas Church

Supplies
- Two 13½×16" pieces of 28-count shell linen
- Cotton embroidery floss
- Needle Necessities overdyed floss
- DMC #5 and #8 pearl cotton
- Desired frame
- 2 rectangles of acid-free foam core to fit the frame

Stitches
Center and stitch the exterior church chart on one piece of linen. Use two plies of floss to work the cross-stitches over two threads of the fabric unless otherwise specified. When working with overdyed floss, complete each stitch before stitching the next one. Complete the cross-stitches first. Refer to the diagrams on *page 20* to work specialty stitches, using one strand of pearl cotton or the number of plies indicated on key.

For the window grid, after working the satin-stitches around the edges of each window, cut and remove the fabric threads from the grid areas, referring to the diagram on *page 20*. Then thread a needle with #8 pearl cotton to work the woven bars and the rosette filling stitch.

Center and stitch the interior church chart on the second piece of linen. Use care to position the chart as indicated on the fabric so the angel and navy square will show through the windows.

Assembly
Press the stitched pieces from the backs. Center the exterior church piece on one rectangle of foam core; mark the approximate location of the window openings. Measure and cut a 3½×5½" rectangular opening for the large window and a 1¼" square opening for the small window. Mount the exterior church piece on the cut foam core. Center and mount the interior church piece on the second piece of foam core. Place the mounted pieces on top of each other in the frame.

Fabric/Needle/Floss Guide

Fabric	Needle Size	Floss: # of Plies
11-Count	24	3 (3X)
14-Count	24–26	2 (2X)
18-Count	26	2 (2X)
22-Count	26	1 (1X)

Christmas Church Angel

Christmas Church Angel Key

CROSS-STITCH (2X)		
ANCHOR	DMC	
002	·	000 White
150	◆	336 Navy
890	∿	680 Old gold
305	✳	725 True topaz
293	▽	727 Pale topaz
275	○	746 Off-white
234	∧	762 Pearl gray
159	⌗	775 Baby blue
024	⊠	776 Medium pink
023	—	818 Pale pink
146	⊓	827 Powder blue

CROSS-STITCH (2X)		
ANCHOR	DMC	
027	◉	899 Rose
292	≡	3078 Lemon
1009	⧄	3770 Ivory

BACKSTITCH (1X)		
ANCHOR	DMC	
403	╱	310 Black – all stitches

STAR STITCH (2X)		
293	✳	727 Pale topaz – stars around angel

Stitch count: *66 high x 35 wide*
Finished design size:
28-count fabric – 4³/₄ x 2¹/₂ inches

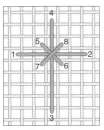

Star Stitch

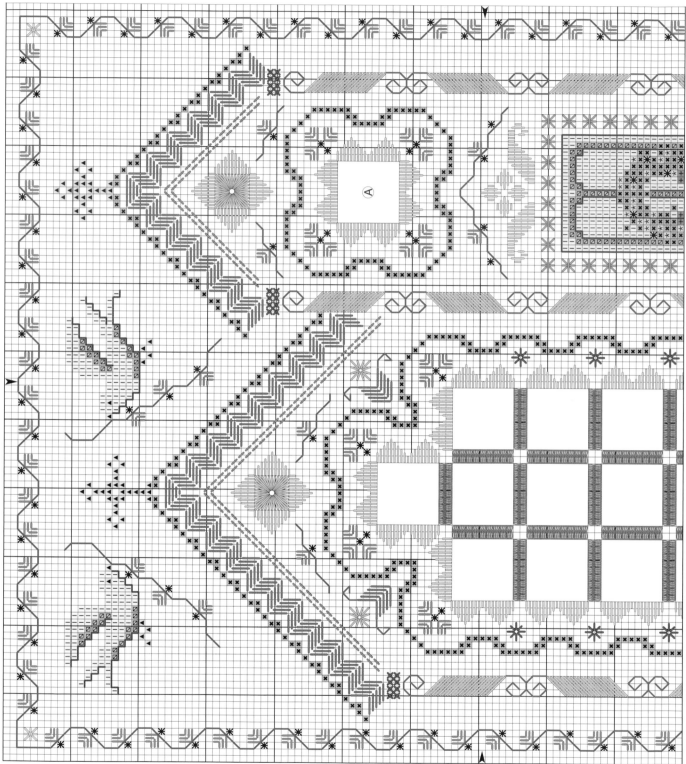

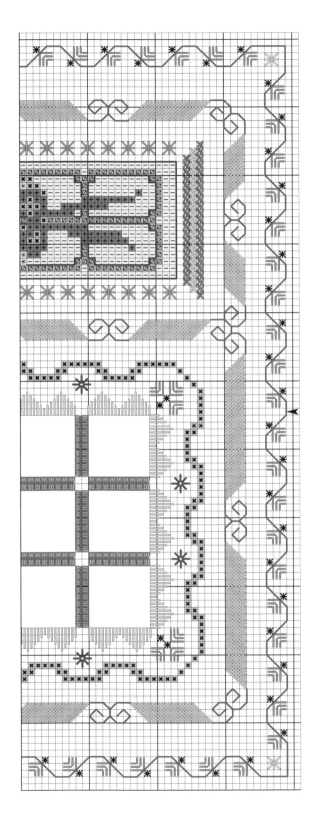

Christmas Church Key

CROSS-STITCH (2X)

ANCHOR		DMC	
1025	+	347	Salmon
590		712	Cream
945	◄	834	Bronze
242	✳	989	Forest green
885	☑	3047	Yellow-beige
	✕	136	Needle Necessities Green with Envy overdyed floss

BACKSTITCH (1X)

590 ╱ 712 Cream #8 pearl cotton – church base and columns

375 ╲ 869 Hazel – door and doves

╱ 136 Needle Necessities Green with Envy overdyed floss – all other stitches

ALGERIAN EYELET (over 10) – (1X)

590 ✴ 712 Cream #5 pearl cotton – center of diamond in gables

ALGERIAN EYELET (over 6) – (1X)

590 ✳ 712 Cream #8 pearl cotton – motifs atop large window

ALGERIAN EYELET (over 4) – (1X)

ANCHOR		DMC	
	✳	136	Needle necessities Green with Envy overdyed floss – corners of border

CABLE STITCH (1X)

590 ╱╱╱ 712 Cream #8 pearl cotton – roof

DIAMOND EYELET (1X)

590 ✳ 136 Needle Necessities Green with Envy overdyed floss – around large window

LONG-ARM CROSS-STITCH (2X)

590 ⨯⨯ 712 Cream – steps under door

885 ⨯⨯⨯ 3047 Yellow-beige – steps under door

RICE STITCH (1X)

590 ⨯⨯ 712 Cream #8 pearl cotton – above 3 church columns

SATIN STITCH (1X)

590 ▥ 712 Cream #5 pearl cotton – pyramid shape blocks around windows and motif above door

SLANTED SATIN STITCH (1X)

ANCHOR		DMC	
590	▨	712	Cream #8 pearl cotton – church base and columns

SMYRNA CROSS-STITCH (over 2) – (2X)

1025 ✳ 347 Salmon – holly berries

SMYRNA CROSS-STITCH (over 4) – (1X)

590 ✳ 712 Cream #8 pearl cotton – detail around door

STRAIGHT STITCH

590 ⫼ 712 Cream #8 pearl cotton – roof and motifs (1X)

⫼ 136 Needle Necessities Green with Envy overdyed floss – leaves (2X)

WOVEN BARS (1X)

590 ▦ 712 Cream #8 pearl cotton – window panes

ROSETTE FILLING STITCH (1X)

590 Ⓐ 712 Cream #8 pearl cotton – window above door

Stitch count: 137 high x 107 wide

Finished design size:
28-count fabric – 9³/₄ x 7²/₃ inches

Christmas Church Stitches

Algerian
Eyelet
(over 4 threads)

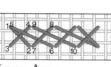
Algerian Eyelet
(over 6 threads)

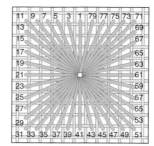
Algerian Eyelet
(over 10 threads)

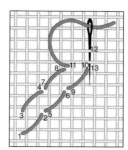
Cable Stitch

Diamond Eyelet

Long-Arm
Cross-Stitch

Rice Stitch

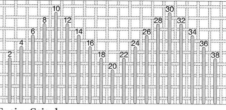
Satin Stitch

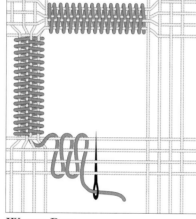
Woven Bars

Smyrna
Cross-Stitch
(over 2 threads)

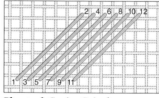
Slanted Satin Stitch

Smyrna
Cross-Stitch
(over 4 threads)

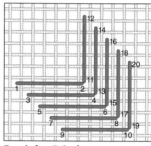
Straight Stitch

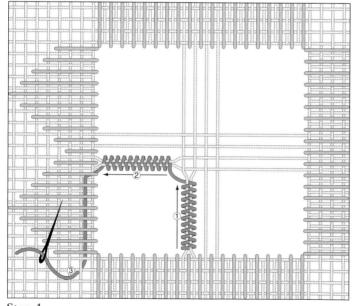
Step 1
Woven Bars with Rosette Filling Stitch

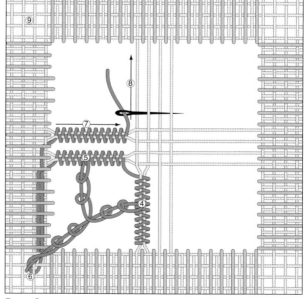
Step 2

Watercolor Santa Boots

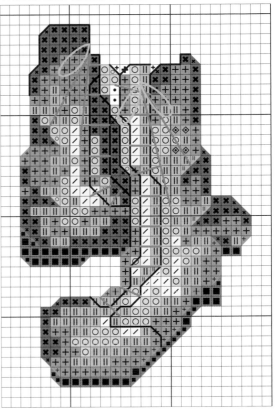

Boot Lacing Detail
See Color Key on pages 22–23.

Watercolor Santa

Supplies
- 12×17½" piece of 14-count white Aida cloth
- Cotton embroidery floss
- Kreinik #4 very fine braid
- DMC metallic floss
- Large-eye tapestry needle
- Desired mat and frame

Stitches
Center and stitch the chart on the Aida cloth. Use three plies of floss to work the stitches over one square of the fabric unless otherwise specified. Use the chart, *above*, to work the boot laces.

For the belt, cut a 25" length each of metallic red, metallic green, and metallic gold floss. Combine the lengths into a single strand. Secure one end of the strand and twist to wind tightly. Holding the ends, fold the strand in half and allow the two halves to twist around each other. Knot one end of the cord; thread the other end into a large-eye tapestry needle. Insert the needle into the front of the fabric at the position marked on the chart. Bring the twisted cord across the fabric back to the position marked on the Santa. Adjust the cord evenly along each side of belt. Knot belt and let it drape around the waist. Referring to the chart for belt placement, *pages 22–23*, use one strand of metallic gold to work couching stitches over the belt at the waist and belt tails. Knot each end of cord. Trim.

Press the stitched piece from the back. Frame as desired.

TIP: Stitching with Metallic Floss

To achieve the best results when working with metallic floss, work with shorter strands than you usually use. Strands approximately 7 or 8 inches long will help prevent the floss from fraying and unraveling as it is pulled through the fabric repeatedly.

When stitching with metallic floss, as with overdyed floss, it is better to complete each cross-stitch as you go rather than work in rows and come back across to complete the stitches.

Watercolor Santa

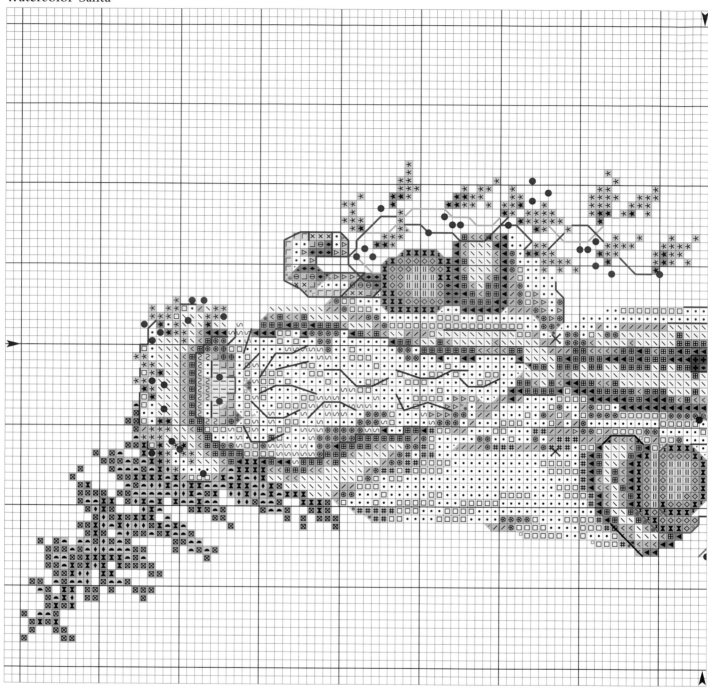

Watercolor Santa Key

CROSS-STITCH (3X)

ANCHOR	DMC		
926			Ecru
002	000		White
352	300	●	Deep mahogany
1049	301	+	Medium mahogany
039	309	●	Dark rose
038	335	⊕	Medium rose
118	340	✦	Medium periwinkle
117	341	/	Light periwinkle
9575	353	2	Dark peach
351	400	✖	Dark mahogany
1047	402	=	Light mahogany
1046	435	⊞	Chestnut
362	437	<	Medium tan
295	726	✱	Light topaz
293	727	▷	Pale topaz
887	739			Pale tan
975	775	□	Light baby blue
307	783	◆	Christmas gold
140	813	✚	Powder blue
1005	816	⊕	Garnet
035	892	⊔	Medium carnation
031	894	▲	Pale carnation
205	912	■	Emerald
152	939	○	Navy
882	945	—	Ivory
1012	948	×	Light peach
073	963	‖	Rose-pink
1070	964	◀	Aqua
355	975	✖	Golden brown
1076	991	#	Dark aquamarine
1072	992	□	Medium aquamarine
144	3325	□	Medium baby blue
1031	3753	⌐	Antique blue
1037	3756	S	Pale baby blue
177	3838	●	Dark lavender-blue
120	3840	⊗	Light lavender-blue
159	3841	▷	Baby blue

BLENDED NEEDLE CROSS-STITCH

267	✱	470 Avocado (1X) and
		015 Kreinik Chartreuse
		#4 very fine braid (1X)
203	⊠	954 Nile green (1X) and
		9194 Kreinik Star green
		#4 very fine braid (1X)
246	★	986 Forest green (1X) and
		009 Kreinik Emerald
		#4 very fine braid (1X)

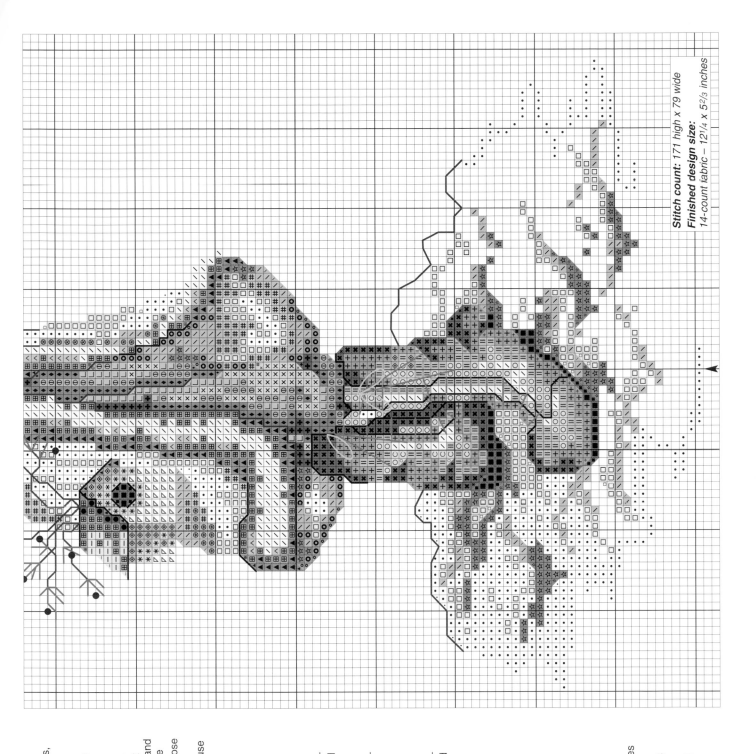

Stitch count: 171 high x 79 wide
Finished design size:
14-count fabric – 12¼ x 5⅔ inches

BACKSTITCH (2X)
352 ╱ 300 Deep mahogany – boots, birdhouse roof, and fur trim on hat and coat
039 ╱ 309 Dark rose – candy cane
117 ╱ 341 Light periwinkle – Santa's eyebrows and beard, bottom of sleeve below candy cane, front of robe between beard and left arm, and candy cane
9575 ╱ 353 Dark peach – Santa's nose
355 ╱ 975 Golden brown – branches above birdhouse
1076 ╱ 991 Dark aquamarine – Santa's mitten

BLENDED NEEDLE BACKSTITCH
038 ╱ 335 Medium rose (1X) and
1005 816 Garnet (1X) – birdhouse hanger
267 ╱ 470 Avocado (1X) and 015 Kreinik Chartreuse #4 very fine braid (1X) – vine in Santa's left hand
205 ╱ 912 Emerald (1X) and 9194 Kreinik Star green #4 very fine braid (1X) – pine needles around birdhouse
246 ╱ 986 Forest green (1X) and 009 Kreinik Emerald #4 very fine braid (1X) – vine in Santa's left hand

FRENCH KNOT (1X wrapped twice)
352 ● 300 Deep mahogany – pinecones around birdhouse
117 ● 341 Light periwinkle – Santa's eyes

BLENDED NEEDLE FRENCH KNOT (wrapped twice)
038 ● 335 Medium rose (1X) and 5270 Metallic red (2X) – berries on hat and vine in left hand

STRAIGHT STITCH (2X)
╱ 5284 Metallic gold – boot laces

LAZY DAISY (2X)
◯ 5284 Metallic gold – boot ties

ATTACHMENT
✗ 5269 Metallic green (1X) and 5270 Metallic red (1X) and 5284 Metallic gold (1X) – Santa's belt

The Holy Family

The Holy Family

Supplies
- 13×16" piece of 14-count dark blue Aida cloth
- Cotton embroidery floss
- Desired frame

Stitches
Center and stitch the chart on the Aida cloth. Use two plies of floss to work the stitches over one square of the fabric unless otherwise specified. Press the stitched piece from the back. Frame as desired.

TIP: Stitching on Dark Fabric
When stitching on dark-colored fabric, place a white cloth in your lap to help you see the weave of the fabric better. It is also helpful to place a small light at your feet.

When framing, put a dark mat or fabric beneath the stitched piece.

The Holy Family Key

CROSS-STITCH (2X)

ANCHOR		DMC	
002	·	000	White
1025	✳	347	Deep salmon
009	⊕	352	Coral
370	◈	434	Chestnut
683	✚	500	Blue-green
210	‖	562	Seafoam
273	◒	645	Dark beaver gray
306	✳	728	Topaz
891	◯	729	Old gold
275	⌐	746	Off-white
159	⊙	775	Baby blue
123	✦	791	Deep cornflower blue
122	⊠	792	Medium cornflower blue
358	▲	801	Medium coffee brown
140	✶	813	Medium powder blue
390	–	822	Beige-gray
127	■	823	Navy
137	◆	824	Deep bright blue
161	⊞	826	Medium bright blue
146	◇	827	Light powder blue
378	✛	841	Beige-brown
381	◧	938	Deep coffee brown
882	▤	945	Ivory
1012	⧄	948	Peach
8581	◹	3022	Medium brown-gray
040	⊠	3023	Light brown-gray
397	⊿	3072	Pale beaver gray

CROSS-STITCH (2X)

ANCHOR		DMC	
1024	▼	3328	Dark salmon
1015	●	3777	Deep terra-cotta
1013	◗	3778	True terra-cotta
868	▢	3779	Pale terra-cotta
899	✩	3782	Mocha
923	⊞	3818	Emerald
891	▽	3822	Straw
324	◪	3853	Dark autumn gold
313	⊛	3854	Medium autumn gold
311	∿	3855	Light autumn gold

HALF CROSS-STITCH
(stitch in direction of symbol)

118	╱	340	Periwinkle (2X)
122	╱	792	Medium cornflower blue (2X)
127	╱	823	Navy (3X)

BACKSTITCH

002	╱	000	White – star (2X)
1025	╱	347	Deep salmon – Mary's shawl (1X)
140	╱	813	Medium powder blue – Mary's robe, head drape of Mary's shawl (1X)
390	╱	822	Beige-gray – border (2X); base of pillars, cat at Joseph's shoulder, cat's ear in lower right corner, top of pillars under chickens, cat, and straw (1X)

BACKSTITCH (2X)

ANCHOR		DMC	
161	╱	826	Medium bright blue – Mary's eye (1X)
378	╱	841	Beige-brown – Mary's hair, donkey's mane (1X)
397	╱	3072	Pale beaver gray – Joseph's hair, mouse ears and head (1X)
311	╱	3855	Light autumn gold – Mary and Joseph's robes, Mary's head piece and cat in lower right corner (1X)
938	╱	938	Deep coffee brown – all other stitches (1X)

FRENCH KNOT

002	●	000	White – baby's halo and stars (2X wrapped once)
009	●	352	Coral – mouse's nose (1X wrapped twice)
381	●	938	Deep coffee brown – chicken's, mouse's and Joseph's eyes (1X wrapped once)
311	●	3855	Light autumn gold – Mary's halo (2X wrapped once)

Stitch count: *136 high x 100 wide*
Finished design size:
14-count fabric – 9 3/4 x 7 1/8 inches

Bright-Colored Santa Ornament

TIP: Using a Mounting Board

When centering a stitched piece on a mounting board, it is helpful to get the top row of stitching in place before pressing the piece to the board. Begin by cutting away a ¼" strip of the protective paper; then align the top of the piece with the board. When you are satisfied that it is squared, peel away the rest of the protective paper and slowly press the rest of the piece to the board from the top down.

Bright-Colored Santa Ornament Key

CROSS-STITCH (3X)

ANCHOR		DMC	
002	⊡	000	White
9046	▲	321	Christmas red
227	✚	701	Christmas green
256	◯	704	Chartreuse
305	▢	725	Topaz
1021	▽	761	Salmon
234	▯	762	Pearl gray
137	✕	798	Delft blue
045	■	814	Dark garnet
043	✚	815	Medium garnet
027	◨	899	Rose
433	◇	996	Electric blue

BACKSTITCH (1X)

403	╱	310	Black–all stitches

Stitch count: 60 high x 60 wide

Finished design size:
28-count fabric – 4¼ x 4¼ inches

Bright-Colored Santa Ornament

Supplies
- 8×8" piece of 28-count white Jubilee fabric
- 4¾" square of felt
- Cotton embroidery floss
- Thick white crafts glue
- 4¾" square self-stick mounting board with foam
- 1 yard of ⅜"-wide black leather lacing

Stitches
Center and stitch the chart on the Jubilee fabric. Use three plies of floss to work the cross-stitches over two threads of fabric. Work the backstitches with one ply.

Assembly
Peel the protective paper backing from the mounting board. Center the foam side on the back of the stitchery; press firmly to apply. Trim fabric to ½" beyond the edge of the mounting board. Fold fabric edges to back, mitering the corners; glue in place.

Beginning at the bottom center of the ornament, glue the lacing around the edge. Trim the excess. Glue the ends of the remaining lacing to the back at the top edge, 1" from the sides. Tie the loop into a knot at the top. Glue the felt to the back. Let the glue dry.

Bright-Colored Santa Ornament

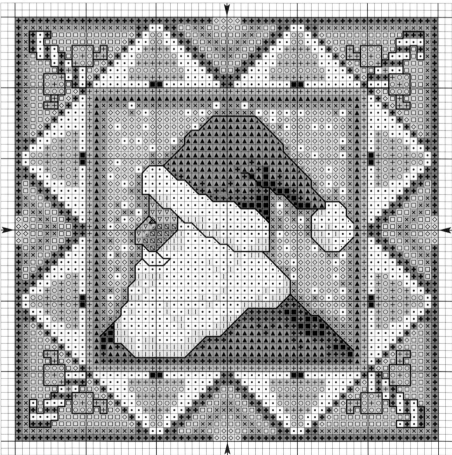

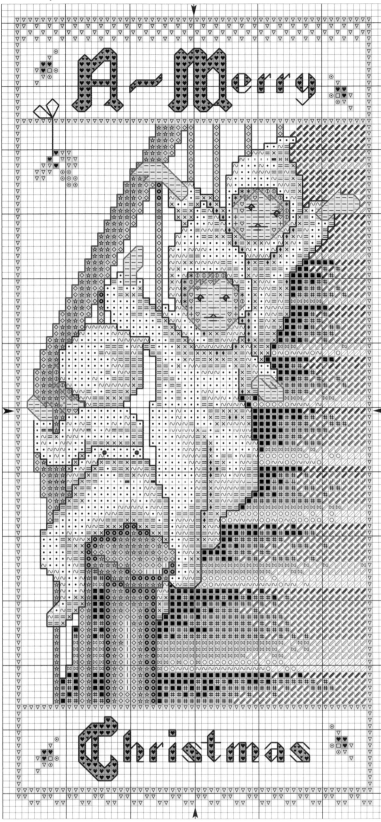

A Merry Christmas

The photograph of the sampler is on page 12.

A Merry Christmas Key

CROSS-STITCH (2X)

ANCHOR		DMC
002	•	000 White
059	♥	326 Deep rose
038	□	335 Medium rose
9575	♡	353 Dark peach
1045	✳	436 Dark tan
362	⏀	437 Medium tan
393	◆	640 Dark beige-gray
392	✕	642 Medium beige-gray
391	=	644 Light beige-gray
882	�	758 Light terra-cotta
390	∼	822 Pale beige-gray
906	■	829 Bronze
1035	◉	930 Dark antique blue
1034	☆	931 Medium antique blue
921	◇	932 True antique blue
1012	–	948 Light peach
887	#	3045 Dark yellow-beige
886	⋈	3046 Medium yellow-beige
885	○	3047 Light yellow-beige
268	▽	3346 Hunter green
266	⊙	3347 Yellow-green
1031	Ⅱ	3753 Pale antique blue

BLENDED NEEDLE CROSS-STITCH

9575	✚	353 Dark peach (1X) and
031		3708 Watermelon (1X)

HALF CROSS-STITCH (1X)
(stitch in direction of symbol)

906	╱	829 Bronze
887	╱	3045 Dark yellow-beige
886	╱	3046 Medium yellow-beige
885	╱	3047 Light yellow-beige

BACKSTITCH (1X)

897	╱	221 Shell pink – lips
5975	╱	356 Medium terra-cotta – faces, hands, and noses
370	╱	434 Chestnut – hair and eyebrows
043	╱	815 Garnet – lettering and hanging ribbon
1035	╱	930 Dark antique blue – banister
360	╱	3031 Mocha – all other stitches

MILL HILL BEAD

●	40123 Cream petite glass beads – pajama buttons

Stitch count: *123 high x 56 wide*

Finished design size:
28-count fabric – 8³⁄4 x 4 inches

A Merry Christmas

Supplies
- 16×20" piece of 28-count antique white Quaker cloth
- Cotton embroidery floss
- Mill Hill 40123 cream petite seed beads
- Desired mat and frame

Stitches
Center and stitch the chart on the fabric. Use two plies of floss to work the stitches over two threads of the fabric unless otherwise specified. Attach seed beads with two plies. Place the finished stitchery face down on a soft towel and carefully press from the back. Frame as desired.

Yuletide Traditions

Cherished holiday symbols
welcome the season year after year.

So much goes into Christmas celebrations! Even before the festive decorating and oh-so-good baking gets underway, gifts begin to accumulate, and special events and visits fill the calendar. These wonderful activities, anticipated from one holiday season to the next, become eagerly awaited family rituals. This selection of cross-stitch projects includes an assortment of favorites: Santas, Christmas trees, nutcrackers, snowmen, and reindeer. As you browse through these familiar holiday designs, let them remind you of special times, and then select one or two to become a part of your yuletide traditions.

A dream-come-true sampler if ever there was one! Clara's Christmas Eve fantasy

of sugarplums and sweets dances across this lively banner. From "The Nutcracker," this stitchery

captures the beloved ballet's most popular characters, including the Nutcracker himself.

Project instructions begin on page 40. Design: Robin Clark.

Nutcracker sweets from the sampler, *opposite,* leap onto center stage as marvelous ornaments. Embroidered on white perforated paper, they finish neatly, quickly when backed with synthetic suede or felt. With just a little more

effort, you can stitch mirror images of the frivolous characters and place one on each side of backing for a two-sided trim. Twirling around on a Christmas tree, holiday garland, or whimsical storybook mobile, these dancing figures will delight children of all ages.

Project instructions begin on page 44.
Designs: Robin Clark.

Some designs have so much appeal, they insist on taking another whirl. From the

Nutcracker sampler, *page 30,* we've charmed the Christmas tree at the top into a sweet pillow.

The diminutive evergreen is embellished with trims and framed with holiday fabrics.

Project instructions begin on page 40. Design: Robin Clark.

What gives this jolly stocking so much folk-art appeal? Could it be the checkerboard trim on Santa's velvet coat? Maybe it's the patchwork heart along the toe. Surely, his breezy mustache and a pocket bulging with candy canes make Santa so endearing!

Project instructions begin on page 45. Design: Robin Kingsley.

Two-tone stockings with bands of pattern echo authentic Scandinavian style. The blend of contemporary and traditional motifs gives the stockings up-to-date charm. Stitched all in white, the designs work up quickly and make good tote-along projects to finish before the holidays.

Project instructions begin on page 48. Designs: Barbara Sestok.

For the all-round crafter, here's a stocking to showcase needlework talents. Complete the four enchanting Santas; then patch them together crazy-quilt style. Use an array of fabrics to create distinctive stockings for the entire family. A flourish of decorative stitches adds the finishing touch.

Project instructions begin on page 36. Design: Barbara Sestok.

Patchwork Quilt Stocking

Santa with Wand

Santa with Heart

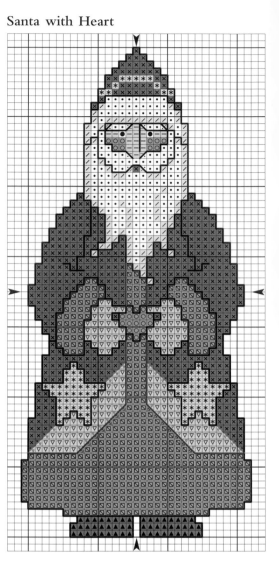

Patchwork Quilt Stocking

Supplies
- 25-count antique ivory Jobelan fabric:
  9×10" piece for Santa with Wand
  8×11" piece for Santa with Heart
  8" square for Santa Ornament
  7×9" piece for Santa Face
- Cotton embroidery floss
- Kreinik very fine braid
- Mill Hill seed beads
- Graph paper
- ½ yard muslin
- ⅝ yard coordinating cotton print fabric
- ¼ yard cotton check fabric for cuff
- Coordinating cotton fabric scraps
- Assorted pearl cottons
- Embroidery needle
- Matching sewing thread

Stitches
Center and stitch each of the charts on the fabric pieces. Use three plies of floss to work the stitches over two threads unless otherwise specified. Attach the seed beads using one ply of matching floss.

Assembly
Enlarge the stocking pattern, *page 39,* on graph paper. Cut out the pattern piece.

Use the stocking pattern to cut one from the muslin, three from the coordinating print fabric—one for the backing, and two for the lining. From the check fabric, cut a 7×20" strip for the cuff.

Referring to the photograph, *page 35* and *left,* trim the Santa Face stitched piece to a rectangle and position it, right

Santa Ornament

Santa Face

Patchwork Quilt Stocking

CROSS-STITCH (2X)

ANCHOR		DMC
352	▲	300 Mahogany
398	╱	415 Pearl gray
046	✕	666 Red
228	⊙	700 Christmas green
256	▽	704 Chartreuse
306	✱	728 Topaz
1041	■	844 Beaver gray
882	─	945 Ivory
1001	◩	976 Golden brown
033	◯	3706 Watermelon
	☆	028 Kreinik citron #4 very fine braid

BLENDED NEEDLE CROSS-STITCH

002	⊡	000 White (2X) and 100HL Kreinik white hi-lustre #4 very fine braid (1X)

BACKSTITCH (1X)

352	╱	300 Mahogany – front trim on Santa with heart coat
1041	╱	844 Beaver gray – all other stitches

STRAIGHT STITCH (2X)

046	╱	666 Red – boot laces

FRENCH KNOT (2X wrapped twice)

403	●	310 Black – eyes on all Santas

STAR STITCH (2X)

002	✳	000 White – stars

MILL HILL SEED BEAD

	◯	00161 Crystal – center of stars around Santa with wand

Santa with Wand stitch count:
63 high x 41 wide
Santa with Wand finished design size:
25-count fabric – 5 x 3¼ inches
Santa with Heart stitch count:
70 high x 33 wide
Santa with Heart finished design size:
25-count fabric – 5⅝ x 2⅝ inches
Santa Ornament stitch count:
46 high x 33 wide
Santa Ornament finished design size:
25-count fabric – 3⅔ x 2⅔ inches
Santa Face stitch count:
39 high x 21 wide
Santa Face finished design size:
25-count fabric – 3⅛ x 1¾ inches

side up, on the muslin stocking foundation; baste in place. Cut a piece of coordinating fabric to place to the left of the Santa Head; press under ½" along the right edge. Position the fabric on the foundation, overlapping about ½" along the stitched piece.

Hand-appliqué the pressed edge in place and baste the remaining edges. Add the remaining stitched pieces and coordinating fabrics, pressing under ½" along the edges that will be on top and basting the edges that will be overlapped. When piecing the fabric, use the photograph on *page 35* for inspiration, cutting shapes that best suit your stocking. After the muslin foundation is covered with fabrics, machine-baste ½" from the stocking edges. Trim the fabric pieces even with the muslin.

To embellish the stocking front, use one strand of pearl cotton in a variety of colors to embroider your choices of stitches to cover the seams, referring to the diagrams, *page 38,* as a guide.

Sew the pieced stocking front to the stocking back, leaving the top edge

open. Trim the seams and clip the curves. Turn the stocking right side out and press.

For the cuff, sew together the short edges of the 7×20" strip to form a loop; press the seam allowances open. Press the cuff in half lengthwise, wrong sides together, matching raw edges and seams. Slip the cuff onto the stocking, aligning the cuff seam with the heel seam, raw edges even. Baste the cuff to the stocking. Use one strand of pearl cotton to embroider buttonhole stitches along the lower edge of the cuff.

Right sides facing, sew the lining pieces together, leaving the top edge open and an opening on one side for turning. Trim the seams and clip the curves; do not turn. Slip the stocking and cuff inside the lining, right sides together. Sew the top edges of the stocking, cuff, and lining together. Trim the seams and turn the stocking right side out.

Slip-stitch the opening closed. Tuck the lining into the stocking. Use a press cloth to carefully press the stocking.

Patchwork Quilt Stocking Stitches

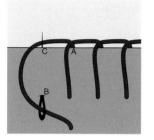

Blanket Stitch

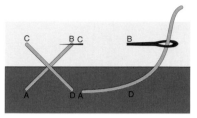

Cross–Stitch

| Step 1 | Step 2 | Step 3 | Step 4 | Step 5 | Step 6 |

Fern Stitch

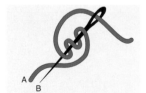

Herringbone

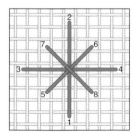

French Knot

Star Stitch

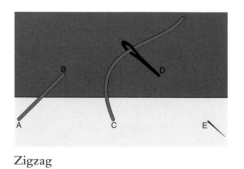

Zigzag

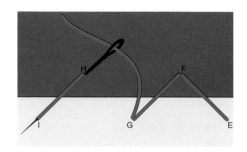

Patchwork Quilt Santa Stocking Pattern

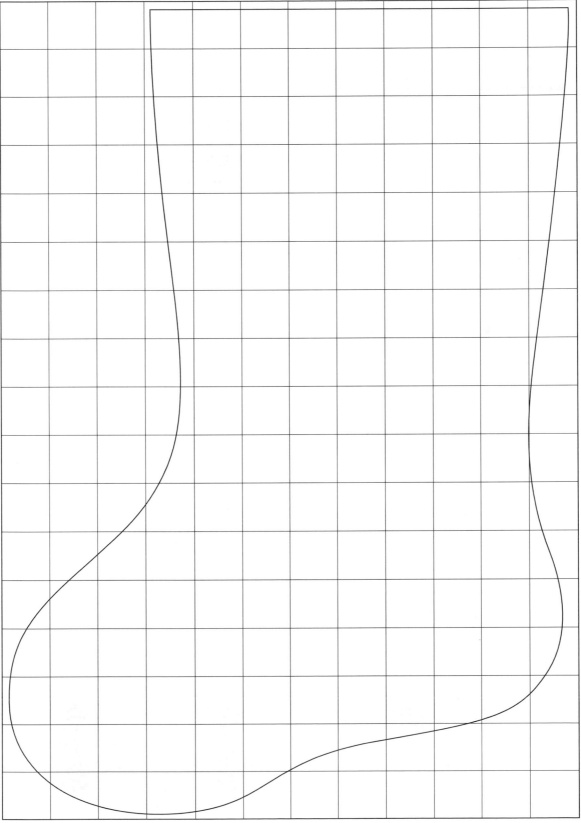

1 Square = 1 Inch

Nutcracker Sweets Banner, Ornaments, and Pillow

The chart and key are on pages 42–44.

Nutcracker Sweets Sampler Banner

Supplies

- 14×19" piece of 14-count light oatmeal Fiddler's Lite fabric
- Cotton embroidery floss; metallic floss
- 10×16¼" piece of lightweight fleece
- ½ yard of beige cotton fabric
- Matching sewing thread
- 8¾" length of ¼"-diameter dowel
- 50" length of ½"-diameter hunter green cord
- 2 purchased 3"-long hunter green tassels

Stitches

Center and stitch the chart on the fabric. Use two plies of floss to work stitches over one square of fabric unless otherwise specified. Lightly press the stitched piece from the back.

Assembly

Centering the design, trim the stitched piece to a 10×16¼" rectangle. Position the fleece on the back of the stitched piece and baste ½" from the outer edges.

From the beige fabric, cut a backing 10×16¼". Right sides facing, sew the stitched piece and backing together, leaving the bottom edge open for turning. Trim the seams and clip the corners. Turn the banner right side out and press. Press under ½" at the bottom edges.

Insert dowel into banner and position it along top edge. Hand-sew dowel in place, sewing only through the backing fabric.

Sew tassels to the banner alongside each lower corner. Sew cording to the side edges of the banner, letting cord ends extend 1½" beyond the lower edge and leaving the excess at the top of the hanger. Tuck the cord ends inside the bottom opening; slip-stitch the opening closed.

Christmas Tree Pillow

Supplies

- 12×11" piece of 22-count Harvest Wheat Almeria fabric
- Cotton embroidery floss; metallic floss
- ⅓ yard green-print cotton fabric
- ⅓ yard red-and-green cotton check fabric
- Matching sewing thread
- 11×10½" rectangle of quilt batting
- Polyester fiberfill

- JHB International shank buttons:
  1¼"-tall cardinal (90031),
  1⅛"- diameter gold star (90095), and
  ¾"-wide red, green, and blue
  packages (22684, 22685, 22686)
- Long needle

Stitches

Center and stitch the tree motif and border from the Nutcracker Sweets Sampler chart, *pages 42–43,* on the fabric. Use three plies of floss to work the stitches over two threads of the fabric unless otherwise specified. Press the stitched piece from the back.

Assembly

Trim the stitched piece to 8×7½", with the top of the tree 1½" below the center top of the fabric. From the green-print fabric, cut two 2½×7½" side sashing strips, two 2½×8" top and bottom sashing strips, and an 11×10½" rectangle for the back. From the red-and-green plaid fabric, cut four 2½" squares and enough 3"-wide bias strips to make a 50" binding strip. All measurements include a ½" seam allowance.

Sew a 2½×7½" side sashing strip to the left and right edges of the stitched piece; press the seam allowances toward the strips. Sew a 2½" checked square to each end of the 2½×8" top and bottom sashing strips; press the seam allowances toward the strips. Sew one pieced strip to the top of the stitched piece and one to the bottom, matching seams, to complete the pillow front. Press seam allowances toward the sashing strips.

Center the batting on the wrong side of the pillow back; then center the pillow front, right side up, on the batting. Sew the layers together, leaving an opening for stuffing. Use polyester fiberfill to stuff the pillow between the batting and pillow backing layers. Sew the opening closed using a zipper foot.

Sew the narrow ends of the 3"-wide binding strips together for a continuous length. Fold the strip in half lengthwise, wrong sides together; press. Raw edges even and using a zipper foot, sew the binding strip along the pillow perimeter, mitering the covers. Fold the binding to the back; slip-stitch the pressed edge of the binding in place to cover the machine stitches.

Use a long needle to sew on the buttons, pulling the thread tightly to slightly indent the pillow for a more full appearance.

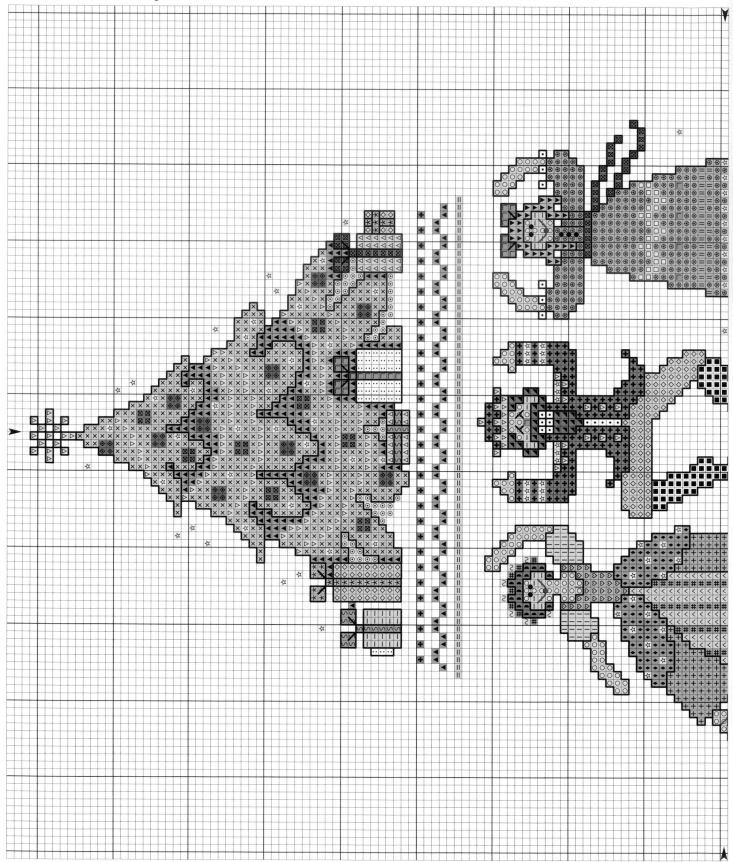

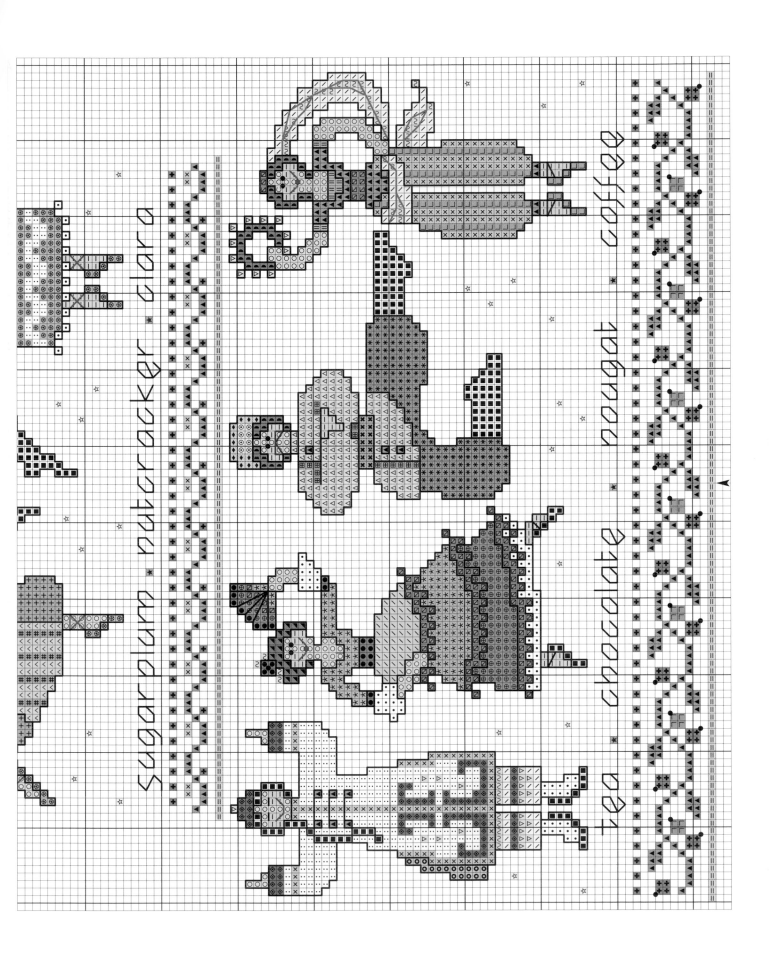

Nutcracker Swets Sampler Key

CROSS-STITCH (2X)

ANCHOR		DMC	
1096	△	3752	Light antique blue
1013	✳	3778	True terra-cotta
1050	◣	3781	Dark mocha
899	◈	3782	Light mocha

METALLIC FLOSS (4X)

		DMC	
5270	◈	Metallic red	
5279	▨	Metallic copper	
5282	▷	Metallic gold	
5283	☆	Metallic silver	
5287	✕	Metallic dark silver	
5288	#	Metallic pink	

BACKSTITCH (2X)

1050	/	3781	Dark mocha – mustache on Nougat

BACKSTITCH (1X)

895	/	223	Medium shell pink – cleavage on Sugarplum and Chocolate
893	/	224	Light shell pink – slipper ties on Sugarplum and Clara
683	/	500	Deep blue-green – inside scarf on Coffee
1027	/	3722	True shell pink – mouths
1019	/	3726	True antique mauve – slipper ties on Coffee
382	/	3371	Black-brown – all other stitches

FRENCH KNOT (2X wrapped once)

382	●	3371	Black-brown – eyes, stems on berries of bottom border
1027	●	3722	True shell pink – mouths

Stitch count: 185 high x 109 wide
Finished design size:
14-count fabric – 13¼ x 7¾ inches

CROSS-STITCH (2X)

ANCHOR		DMC	
002	·	000	White
897	✚	221	Deep shell pink
895	⌐	223	Medium shell pink
893	⊕	224	Light shell pink
271	□	225	Pale shell pink
403	■	310	Black
1079	⊠	315	Dark antique mauve
1018	▷	316	Medium antique mauve
1014	●	355	Dark terra-cotta
5975	⊕	356	Medium terra-cotta
683	◀	500	Deep blue-green
878	✕	501	Dark blue-green
877	‖	502	Medium blue-green
875	⊿	503	True blue-green
1042	/	504	Pale blue-green
8581	◆	646	Medium beaver gray
1040	⊙	647	True beaver gray
874	◉	676	Old gold
9575	╲	758	Light terra-cotta
1021	|	761	Salmon
1016	◁	778	Pale antique mauve
1034	✳	931	Medium antique blue
921	⊞	932	True antique blue
4146	○	950	Rose-beige
360	◥	3031	Deep mocha
903	▶	3032	Medium mocha
871	═	3041	Medium antique violet
870	✚	3042	Light antique violet
292	◌	3078	Lemon
382	★	3371	Black-brown
1027	⌐	3722	True shell pink
1019	⑤	3726	True antique mauve
872	◆	3740	Dark antique violet
869	▭	3743	Pale antique violet

Nutcracker Ornaments

The chart is on pages 42–43; the key is above.

Supplies for each ornament

- 4" square of 14-count antique white perforated paper
- Cotton embroidery floss
- Metallic floss
- 5" square of synthetic suede or felt
- Crafts glue
- 8" length of ⅛"-wide white satin ribbon

Stitches

Center and stitch a Nutcracker Sweets motif from the Sampler chart, *pages 42–43*, on the perforated paper. Use three plies of floss to work the stitches unless otherwise specified.

Assembly

Trim the stitched piece one square beyond the stitched area of the design. Center the stitched piece on the synthetic suede and glue in place. Trim the excess suede a scant ¼" beyond the perforated paper edges. For the hanging loop, fold the ribbon in half and knot the ends together. Sew the ribbon to the top center back of the ornament.

Folk Art Santa Stocking

Supplies

- Two 13×19" pieces of 28-count Spun Silver or Star Sapphire linen
- Cotton embroidery floss
- Erasable fabric marker
- ½ yard of red-print cotton fabric
- ½ yard of lightweight fleece
- 1 yard of ³⁄₁₆"-diameter cording
- Matching sewing thread

Stitches

Find the center of the fabric and the chart. Begin stitching there. Use two plies of floss to work the stitches over two threads of the fabric unless otherwise specified. Carefully press the stitched piece from the back.

Assembly

Use the erasable fabric marker to draw the stocking outline, as indicated by the dashed line on the chart. Cut out ½" beyond the marked line. Use the stocking as a pattern to cut a matching linen backing, two lining pieces from red-print fabric, and two pieces of lightweight fleece. From the remaining red-print fabric, cut a 1¼×5" hanger strip, and enough 1¾"-wide bias strips to make a 36" length of piping.

Sew the short ends of the 1¾"-wide bias strips together to make a continuous length. Center the cording lengthwise on the wrong side of the piping strip. Fold the fabric around the cording, long edges even. Use a zipper foot to sew through fabric layers close to the cording.

Folk Art Santa Stocking

The chart and key are on pages 46–47.

Baste the fleece to the wrong side of the stocking front and back. Raw edges even, baste the piping around the sides and foot of the stocking front. Right sides together, sew the stocking front to the back along the basting lines, leaving the top edge open. Trim the seams and clip the curves. Turn the stocking right side out; press.

For the hanger, press under ⅜" along each long edge of the 1¼×5" hanger strip. Fold the strip in half lengthwise, aligning pressed edges; press again. Sew the long edges together opposite the fold. Fold the strip in half to form a loop. Baste the ends to the top outer corner of the toe side of the stocking.

Right sides facing, sew the lining pieces together with a ½" seam allowance, leaving the top edge open and an opening on one side for turning. Trim the seams and clip the curves; do not turn. Right sides together, slip the stocking inside the lining. Sew top edges of stocking and lining together; turn right side out. Slip-stitch opening closed. Tuck the lining into the stocking; press.

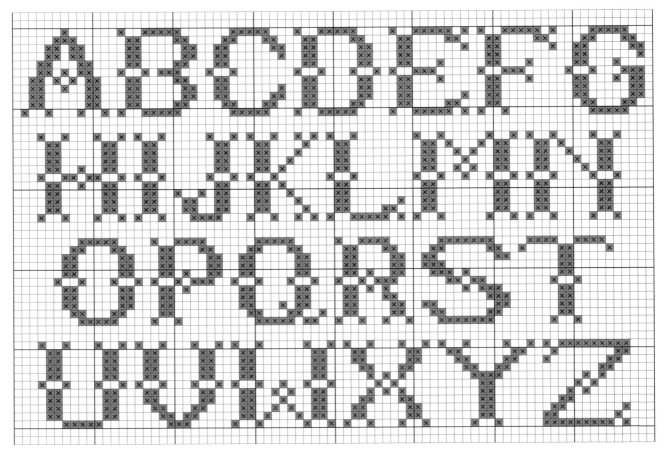

Folk Art Santa Stocking Key

CROSS-STITCH (2X)

ANCHOR		DMC	
926	•		Ecru
1025	✕	347	Deep salmon
370	+	434	Chestnut
305	╱	725	Topaz
868	I	754	Peach
1022	⊕	760	True salmon
307	✱	783	Christmas gold
358	⊠	801	Coffee brown
045	✚	814	Garnet
1044	◀	895	Dark hunter green
274	○	928	Gray-blue
268	#	3346	Light hunter green
264	I	3348	Yellow-green
382	■	3371	Black-brown
1023	II	3712	Medium salmon
169	◁	3760	Medium Wedgwood blue
164	◆	3842	Deep Wedgwood blue

BACKSTITCH

1025	╱	347	Deep salmon – candy cane and peppermint stick stripes
268	╱	3346	Light hunter green – peppermint stick stripes
382	╲	3371	Black-brown – all other stitches

STRAIGHT STITCH

| 382 | ╲ | 3371 | Black-brown – heart, trim on pockets and bottom of Santa's robe |

Stitch count: *215 high x 122 wide*

Finished design size:
28-count fabric – 15³⁄₈ x 8³⁄₄ inches

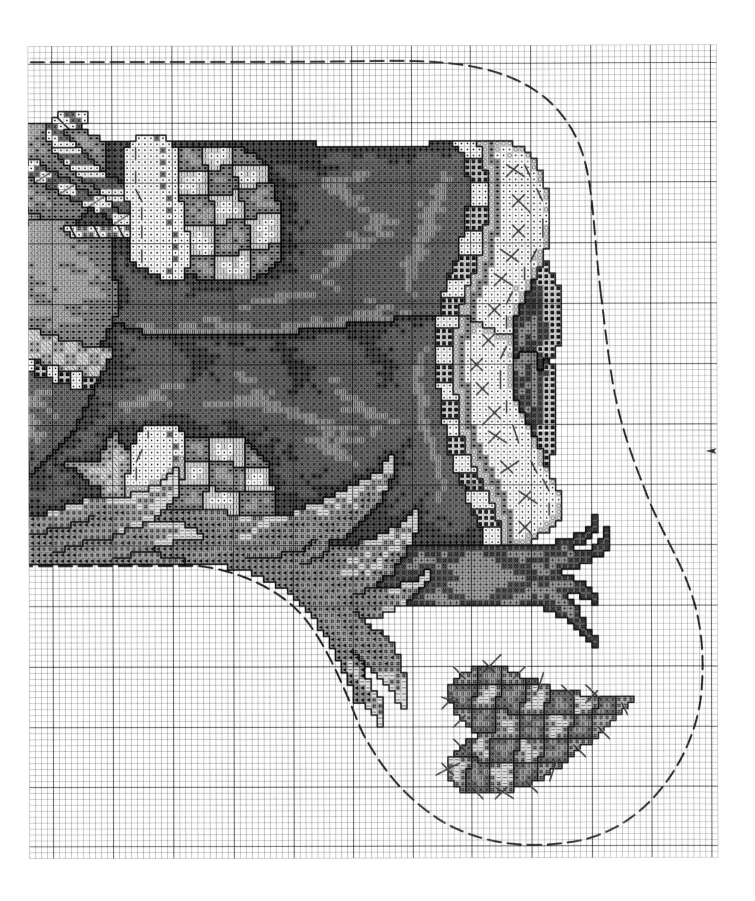

Whitework Stockings

Joy Stocking

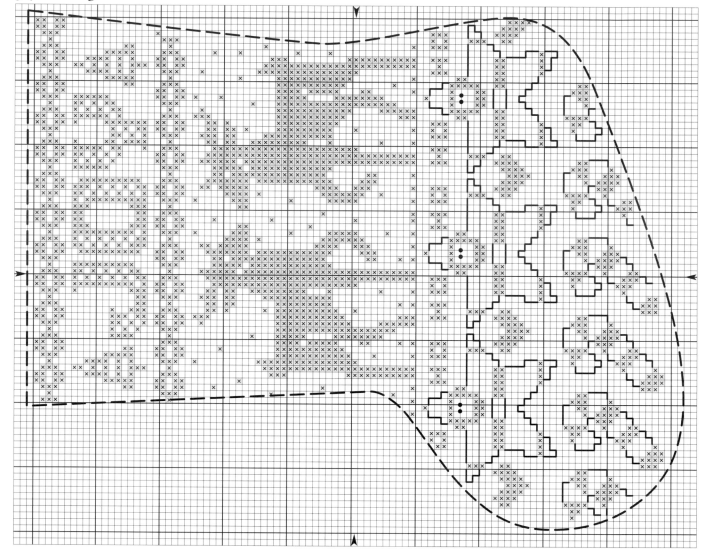

Whitework Stockings

Supplies for each stocking
- Two 12×14" pieces of 25-count Christmas Red or Victorian Christmas Green Lugana fabric
- Cotton embroidery floss
- Erasable fabric marker
- ⅓ yard of print cotton fabric
- 1 yard of purchased white sew-in piping
- 10" length of ⅜"-wide white ribbon
- ½"-diameter white button
- Matching sewing thread

Stitches
Find the center of the desired chart, *above* or *opposite*, and the fabric. Begin stitching there. Use two plies of floss to work the stitches over two threads of the fabric unless otherwise specified. Press the stitched piece from the back.

Assembly
Use the erasable fabric marker to draw the stocking outline as indicated by the dashed line on the chart. Cut out ½" beyond the marked line. Use the stocking as a pattern to cut a matching red or green fabric back and two lining pieces from the print fabric.

Raw edges even and using a zipper foot, baste the piping around the sides and foot of the stocking front. Right sides together, sew the stocking front to the back along the basting lines, leaving the top edge open. Trim the seams and clip the curves. Turn the stocking right

Noel Stocking

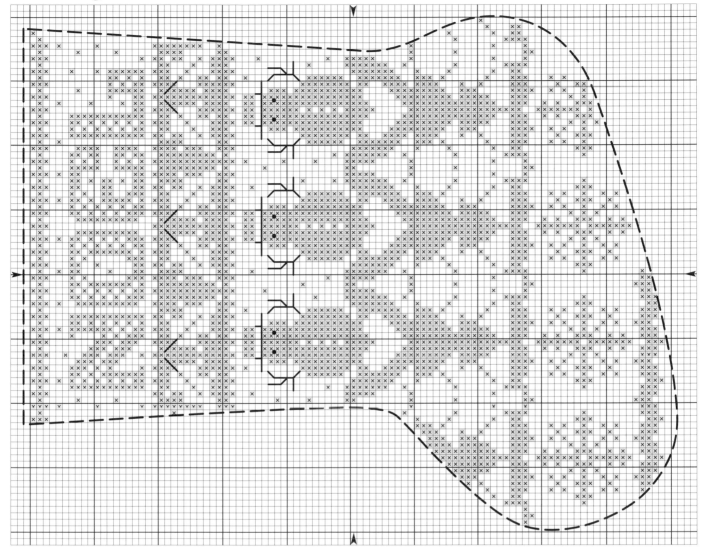

side out and lightly press. Baste piping around top edge of the stocking, raw edges even.

Right sides facing, sew lining pieces together with a ½" seam allowance, leaving the top edge open and an opening on one side for turning. Trim the seams and clip the curves; do not turn. Slip the stocking inside the lining right sides together. Sew the top edges of the stocking and lining together; turn right side out. Slip-stitch the opening closed. Tuck the lining into the stocking and press.

For the hanger, fold the white ribbon to form a loop, overlapping the ribbon about 1½" from the ends. Pin the ribbon to the stocking, overlapping at the top right side; sew in place with a button.

Joy and Noel Stockings Key

ANCHOR DMC

CROSS-STITCH (2X)

002 ☒ 000 White

BACKSTITCH

002 ╱ 000 White – all stitches

FRENCH KNOT (1X wrapped twice)

002 ● 000 White – Santa eyes, snowman eyes

Reindeer stocking stitch count:
99 high x 78 wide

Reindeer finished design size:
25-count fabric – 8 x 6¼ inches

Snowman stocking stitch count:
99 high x 79 wide

Snowman stocking finished design size:
25-count fabric – 8 x 6⅜ inches

Merry and Bright

Hand-stitch little treasures to decorate
trees, wreaths, walls, and mantels.

The merriest Christmases are those

when you craft with lots of Xs and

Ooooohs! Thanks to the wonderful

collection of cross-stitch projects on

the next few pages, you'll be blessed

with plenty of both. Choose from

adorable Santa and mitten ornaments,

an angelic tree topper, a toy-filled

stocking, and a sleighful more. Whether

you stitch holiday gifts to surprise family and friends or to

decorate your own home, you'll make the season brighter

and merrier for all with your artful cross-stitch creations.

Have a joyful time choosing and stitching favorites to give

as gifts or keep for yourself.

An exuberant mix of pattern and stitches star on this cheerful piece of patchwork. A nine-patch of engaging holiday motifs, the blocks are cross-stitched, then bordered with plain and fancy stitches. Embroidery stars, running stitches, and zigzags highlight the familiar symbols.

Project instructions begin on page 69. Design: Gail Bussi.

Individual holiday motifs borrowed from the pillow, *opposite,* merit distinction as tiny stuffed ornaments to hang on the tree or to tie onto packages. Fill these miniature trims with scented fiberfill for a special touch.

Project instructions begin on page 69.
Designs: Gail Bussi.

Express good wishes this Christmas. Colorful stitches are worked on purchased Aida cloth stockings and embellished with beads, charms, and satin ribbons through the eyelets. As an alternative, personalize the little socks with short names in place of the words, and use them as gift tags. They'll be a delight to make—and to receive.

Project instructions begin on page 62.
Design: Barbara Sestok.

Affix this Santa star trio to an arrangement of greenery, and watch the magic! The wands suggest a little bit of wizardry in these Santas. Except for a change in color, each one is worked identically on perforated plastic. For light-catching twinkle, attach beads, bells, and sparkles.

Project instructions begin on page 58.
Design: Barbara Sestok.

Invite the sweetest angel to take flight from the sampler, *opposite,* and alight on the top of your tree. The slender Scandinavian-inspired topper is worked on pastel Aida; otherwise, all stitching remains the same as the sampler. To finish, add a seam allowance and cut around the stitched shape. Assemble with backing and piping for a lightweight yet sturdy ornament.

Project instructions begin on page 60.
Design: Mari McDonald.

This heavenly duo sings praises attired in old-world elegance. With wings shaped like stringed lutes, the pair lifts hands and eyes toward holly-trimmed arches. A textured linen background anchors the stitchery, and a gold frame complements the gleaming stitched border.

Project instructions begin on page 60. Design: Mari McDonald.

Why fill this Christmas stocking? This stitched treasure is treat enough. The

toyland design will inspire children to dream of the wonderful gifts delivered on Christmas

Eve. Even the letters are embellished with tiny dangling jingle bells.

Project instructions begin on page 64. Design: Barbara Sestok.

The yuletide custom of gift giving began when the Magi presented gold, frankincense, and myrrh to the Christ Child. Today, we lavish our loved ones with gifts such as those shown here. Stitched with love, this little trio is gift, gift wrap, and ornament all in one.

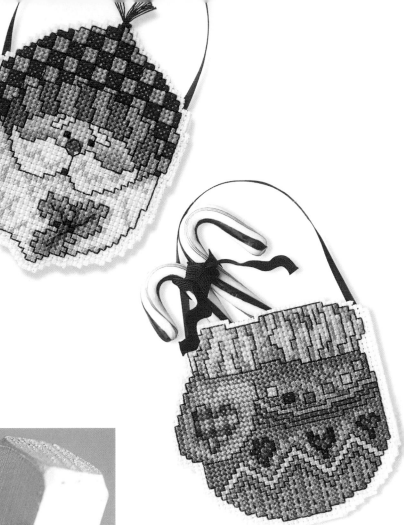

Crafted on Aida cloth, each design becomes a pocket when folded in half along one side and hand-stitched on the remaining side and bottom. Attach a ribbon handle; then tuck tiny treats inside to place on a tree, chair back, or package.

Project instructions begin on page 72.
Designs: Robin Kingsley.

Magical Santa Ornaments

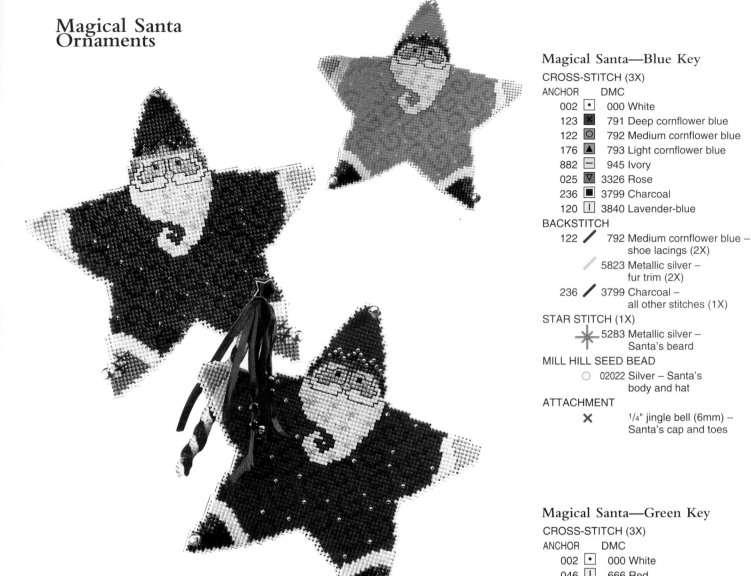

Magical Santa Ornaments

Supplies for each ornament
- 7" square of 14-count white perforated plastic
- Cotton embroidery floss
- Metallic floss
- Mill Hill seed beads
- 3—6mm gold jingle bells
- 1—4" length each of red and white pipe cleaners
- 28" piece of 4mm red silk ribbon
- 9 assorted 4.5mm metallic beads
- 13mm gold star bead

Stitches
Center and stitch the chart on perforated plastic. Use three plies of floss to work the stitches unless otherwise specified. Attach the beads with two plies of matching floss.

Assembly
Trim the stitched piece one square beyond the stitched area. Attach the jingle bells to the boots and the top of the hat with three plies of floss.

To make the wand, twist together the 4" lengths of red and white pipe cleaners. For the streamers, cut four 7" lengths of red silk ribbon. Thread a single 4.5mm metallic bead onto the center of the ribbon lengths to combine the lengths. Thread the ribbon ends through the gold star bead.

To attach the streamers, slip the gold star bead onto one end of the wand. Pull the ribbon ends, pulling the metallic bead against the wand; position the gold star against the metallic bead. Thread two metallic beads onto pairs of ribbons. Sew the wand to Santa's hand with white floss.

Magical Santa—Blue Key

CROSS-STITCH (3X)

ANCHOR		DMC	
002	·	000	White
123	✖	791	Deep cornflower blue
122	◎	792	Medium cornflower blue
176	▲	793	Light cornflower blue
882	⊟	945	Ivory
025	▽	3326	Rose
236	■	3799	Charcoal
120	◫	3840	Lavender-blue

BACKSTITCH

122	╱	792	Medium cornflower blue – shoe lacings (2X)
	╱	5823	Metallic silver – fur trim (2X)
236	╱	3799	Charcoal – all other stitches (1X)

STAR STITCH (1X)

	✳	5283	Metallic silver – Santa's beard

MILL HILL SEED BEAD

	○	02022	Silver – Santa's body and hat

ATTACHMENT

	✕		¼" jingle bell (6mm) – Santa's cap and toes

Magical Santa—Green Key

CROSS-STITCH (3X)

ANCHOR		DMC	
002	·	000	White
046	◫	666	Red
923	✖	699	Dark Christmas green
239	◎	702	Light Christmas green
043	▲	815	Garnet
882	⊟	945	Ivory
025	▽	3326	Rose
236	■	3799	Charcoal

BACKSTITCH

239	╱	702	Light Christmas green – shoe lacings (2X)
	╱	5824	Metallic dark gold – fur trim (2X)
236	╱	3799	Charcoal – all other stitches (1X)

STAR STITCH (1X)

	✳	5283	Metallic silver – Santa's beard

MILL HILL SEED BEAD

	○	00557	Gold – Santa's body and hat

ATTACHMENT

	✕		¼" jingle bell (6mm) – Santa's cap and toes

Magical Santa Ornaments
Use this chart for all three colors. See the individual key for each color.

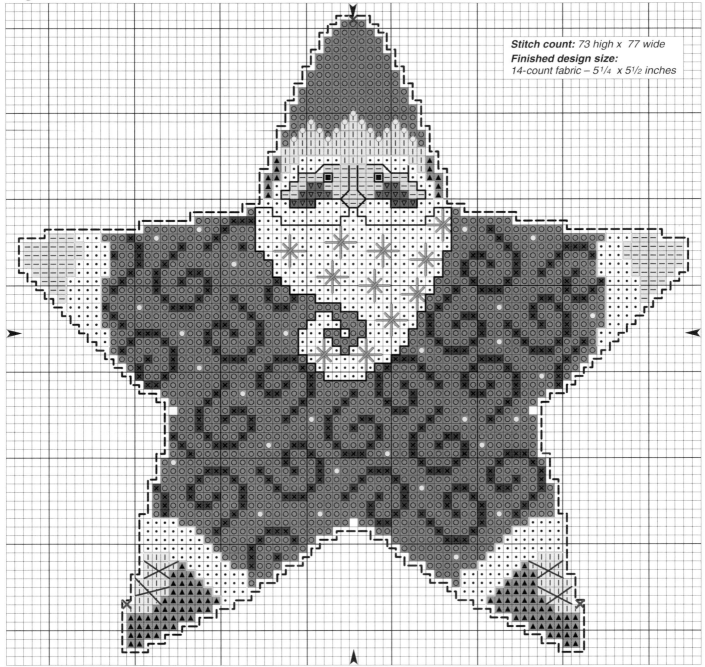

Stitch count: 73 high x 77 wide
Finished design size:
14-count fabric – 5¼ x 5½ inches

Magical Santa—Red Key

CROSS-STITCH (3X)

ANCHOR		DMC
002	•	000 White
046	○	666 Red
923	▲	699 Dark Christmas green
239	I	702 Light Christmas green
043	✕	815 Garnet
882	—	945 Ivory
025	▽	3326 Rose
236	■	3799 Charcoal

BACKSTITCH (2X)

046	╱	666 Red – shoe lacings
	╱	5824 Metallic dark gold – fur trim

BACKSTITCH (1X)

ANCHOR		DMC
236	╱	3799 Charcoal – all other stitches

STAR STITCH (1X)

	✳	5283 Metallic silver – Santa's beard

MILL HILL SEED BEAD

	○	00557 Gold – Santa's body and hat

ATTACHMENT

	✕	¼" jingle bell (6mm) – Santa's cap and toes

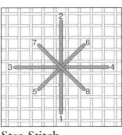

Star Stitch

Angel Sampler and Tree Topper

Angel Sampler

Supplies
- 11½×13" piece of 35-count natural brown linen
- Cotton embroidery floss; Kreinik very fine braid
- Mill Hill seed beads
- Desired frame

Stitches
Center and stitch the chart on linen. Use two plies of floss to work the stitches over two threads of the fabric unless otherwise specified. Attach the seed beads using one ply of matching floss. Press the stitched piece from the back. Frame as desired.

Angel Tree Topper

Supplies
- Two pieces of 9×16" piece of 10-count bone Tula fabric
- Cotton embroidery floss
- Kreinik very fine braid
- Mill Hill seed beads
- Erasable fabric marker
- 7×12" piece of lightweight fleece
- ¼ yard of cream cotton fabric
- ¾ yard of purchased red sew-in piping
- Matching sewing thread

Stitches
Center and stitch the girl angel motif from the Angel Sampler chart, *opposite,* on the fabric. Use three plies of floss to work the stitches over one square of the fabric unless otherwise specified. Press from the back.

Assembly
Referring to the photograph, *above,* use the erasable fabric marker to draw an outline about ½" beyond the stitching.

Center the fleece on the back of the stitched piece. Baste the stitched piece to the fleece on the marked line. Cut out ½" beyond the basting line. Use the trimmed stitched piece as a pattern to cut matching Tula fabric backing and two lining pieces from cotton.

Raw edges even, use a zipper foot to baste the piping around the sides and top. Right sides together, using a zipper foot, sew the front to the backing along the basting lines, leaving the bottom edge open. Trim the seams and clip the curves. Turn the topper right side out; press.

Right sides facing, sew the lining pieces together with a ½" seam allowance, leaving the bottom edge open and an opening on one side for turning. Trim the seams and clip the curves; do not turn. Slip topper inside the lining with right sides together. Sew the bottom edges of the topper and lining together; turn right side out. Slip-stitch the opening closed. Tuck the lining into the topper. Press carefully.

Angel Sampler and Angel Sampler Key

CROSS-STITCH (2X)		
ANCHOR	DMC	
403	■	310 Black
019	✕	349 Coral
5975	+	356 Terra-cotta
398	◇	415 Pearl gray
359	#	433 Chestnut
860	=	522 Olive drab
890	▽	680 Dark old gold
868	○	754 Medium peach
358	▢	801 Coffee brown
022	♥	814 Dark garnet
020	◉	816 Light garnet

CROSS-STITCH (2X)		
ANCHOR	DMC	
380	●	838 Beige-brown
862	◆	934 Deep pine green
861	⊕	935 Dark pine green
1012	−	948 Light peach
397	I	3072 Beaver gray
382	▲	3371 Black-brown
891	╱	3822 Straw
901	★	3829 Deep old gold
001	·	B5200 Bright white
	✳	202HL Kreinik Aztec gold #4 very fine braid

BACKSTITCH (1X)		
ANCHOR	DMC	
403	╱	310 Black – center crease on boy's trousers
5975	╱	356 Terra-cotta – hands
398	╱	415 Pearl gray – wings
380	╱	838 Beige-brown – part in boy's hair
382	╱	3371 Black-brown – eyes
891	╱	3822 Straw – part in girl's hair
	╱	202HL Kreinik Aztec gold #4 very fine braid – lattice work on gown, trim on boy's jacket and trousers

MILL HILL SEED BEAD

○ 00557 Gold – buttons on the boy's jacket and skirt of the girl's gown

Sampler stitch count:
110 high x 93 wide

Sampler finished design size:
35-count fabric – 6¼ x 5⅓ inches

Tree topper stitch count:
102 high x 40 wide

Tree topper finished design size:
10-count fabric – 10¼ x 4 inches

Peace and Noel Mini-Stockings

Peace Mini-Stocking Key

CROSS-STITCH (3X)

ANCHOR		DMC
013	◉	349 Coral
275	•	746 Off-white
146	✚	827 Powder blue
227	✘	911 Medium emerald
882	▬	945 Ivory
297	╱	973 Canary
1015	♥	3777 Deep terra-cotta
868	◖	3779 Pale terra-cotta
306	▽	3820 Straw
1048	▢	3826 Golden brown
	☆	002 Kreinik Gold #4 very fine braid
	✳	210 Kreinik Gold dust #4 very fine braid

BLENDED NEEDLE CROSS-STITCH

013	◩	349 Coral (2X) and
1015		3777 Deep terra-cotta (1X)

BACKSTITCH

161	╱	826 Bright blue – angel's wings (1X)
229	╱	909 Dark emerald – lettering (2X)
	╱	210 Kreinik Gold dust #4 very fine braid – halo and star (1X)
236	╱	3799 Charcoal – all other stitches (1X)

MILL HILL SEED BEAD

●		62013 Frosted red red – lettering and holly

ATTACHMENT

✕		Homespun Elegance gold star – stocking background

Stitch count: *49 high x 31 wide*
Finished design size:
14-count fabric – 3¹/₂ x 2¹/₄ inches

Peace and Noel Mini-Stockings

Supplies for each stocking

- Purchased 14-count white Aida cloth stocking
- Cotton embroidery floss
- Kreinik very fine braid
- Mill Hill seed beads
- Homespun elegance gold star charms
- ⅛"-wide satin ribbon

Stitches

Center and stitch the desired chart on the stocking. Use three plies of floss to work the stitches over one square of the fabric unless otherwise specified. Attach the seed beads and star charms with two plies of matching floss. Press the stitched piece from the back. For the hanging loop, thread ⅛"-wide ribbon through the hole at the top heel side of the stocking; knot the ribbon ends together.

French Knot Phobia?

Do you have French knot phobia? Practice making the knots at the edge of your fabric or on another piece of it. Remember to bring your needle down at least one thread over from where you came up. Tighten the twists. The floss will slide through the wrapped thread to make the knot. Soon you'll wonder why you were ever in fear of French knots.

Peace Mini-Stocking

Noel Mini-Stocking

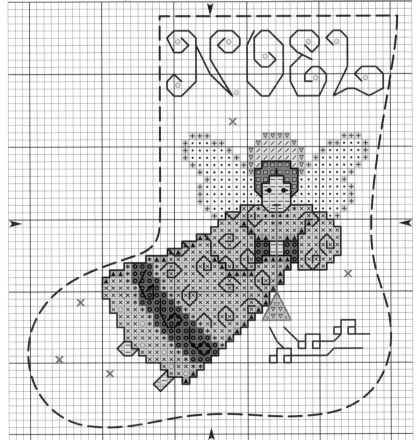

Noel Mini-Stocking Key

CROSS-STITCH (3X)

ANCHOR		DMC	
013	◉	349	Coral
275	•	746	Off-white
146	⊞	827	Powder blue
229	▲	909	Dark emerald
227	✕	911	Medium emerald
882	−	945	Ivory
297	╱	973	Canary
306	▽	3820	Straw
1048	▣	3826	Golden brown
	✳	210	Kreinik Gold dust #4 very fine braid

BACKSTITCH

013	╱	349 Coral – lettering (2X); angel's mouth and gown (1X)
	╱	210 Kreinik Gold dust #4 very fine braid – horn (1X)
236	╱	3799 Charcoal – musical notes and lines (2X); all other stitches (1X)

FRENCH KNOT WITH SHORT STITCH
(2X wrapped once)

236	●	3799 Charcoal – angel's eyes

MILL HILL SEED BEAD

	○	00557 Gold – angel's gown and "Noel"

ATTACHMENT

	✕	Homespun Elegance gold star – stocking background

Stitch count: 50 high x 39 wide
Finished design size:
14-count fabric – 3²/₃ x 2⁷/₈ inches

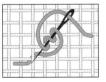

French Knot
with Short
Stitch

Attaching Beads
Diagram

Traditional Toys Stocking

The chart and key are on pages 66–68.
The alphabet chart is opposite.

Stitches

Find the center of the chart and the center of the Aida cloth; begin stitching there. Use two plies of floss to work the stitches over one square of fabric unless otherwise specified. Attach the Treasures and the seed and bugle beads with two plies of matching floss. To attach the buttons, bring matching thread to the front through a buttonhole, pick up a gold seed bead, and return to the back through the same hole. Press the stitched piece from the back.

Assembly

Use the erasable fabric marker to draw the stocking outline as indicated by the dashed line on the chart. Cut out ½" beyond the marked line. Use the stocking as a pattern to cut a matching backing, two lining pieces from coordinating print fabric, and two from lightweight fleece. From the remaining print fabric, cut a 2×6½" hanger strip and a 1¾×44" strip for piping.

Center the cording lengthwise on the inside of the piping strip. Fold the fabric around the cording, long edges even. Use a zipper foot to sew through both layers, encasing the cording.

Baste the fleece to the wrong side of the stocking front and back. Raw edges even, baste the piping around stocking sides and foot. Right sides together, sew the stocking front to the back along the basting lines, leaving the top edge open. Trim the seams; clip the curves. Turn the stocking right side out; press.

For the hanger, press under ½" on each long edge of the 2×6½" hanger strip. Fold the strip in half lengthwise, aligning pressed edges; press again. Sew together the long edges opposite the fold. Fold the strip in half to form a loop. Baste the ends to the top outer corner on the heel side of the stocking.

Right sides facing, sew the lining pieces together with a ½" seam allowance, leaving the top edge open and an opening on one side for turning. Trim the seams and clip the curves; do not turn. Slip the stocking inside the lining, right sides together. Sew the top edges of the stocking and the lining together; turn right side out. Slip-stitch the opening closed. Tuck the lining into the stocking; press carefully.

Traditional Toys Stocking

Supplies
- 15×19" piece of 14-count mocha soft Aida cloth
- Cotton embroidery floss
- Kreinik very fine braid
- Mill Hill seed and bugle beads
- Mill Hill Treasures
- Erasable fabric marker
- Buttons: 8—¼"-diameter yellow, 4—⅝"-diameter red, and 1—1"-diameter red
- ½ yard of coordinating print cotton fabric
- ½ yard of lightweight fleece
- 1¼ yard of ³⁄₁₆"-diameter cording
- Matching sewing thread

Traditional Toys Stocking Alphabet

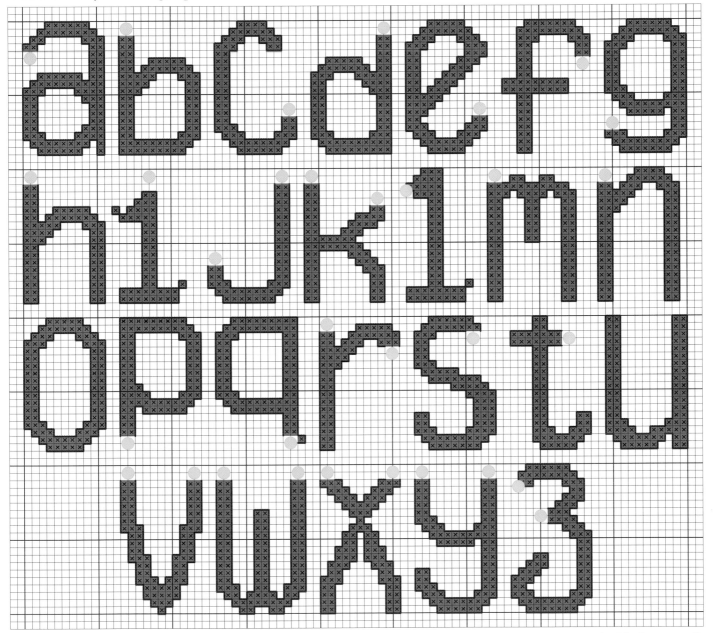

See Color Key on page 68.

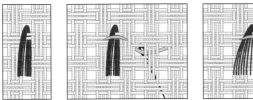

Tassel Diagram

Attaching Beads Diagram

Bow Bead Diagram

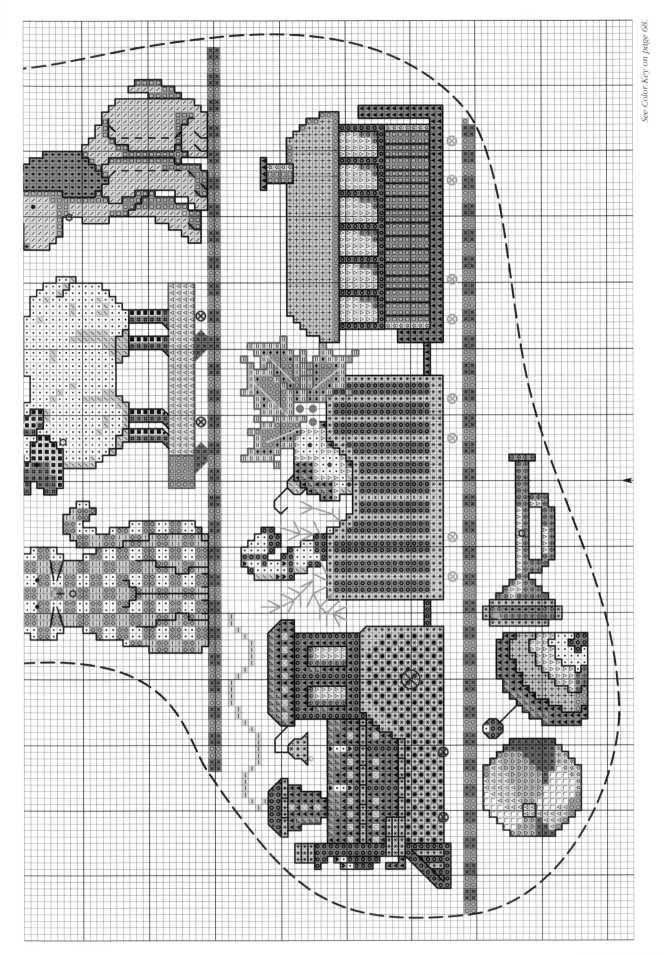

See Color Key on page 68.

Traditional Toys Stocking Key

CROSS-STITCH (2X)

ANCHOR		DMC	
1094	▷	151	Dusty rose
939	◇	156	Lavender-blue
343	∣	159	Gray-blue
280	▤	166	Moss green
374	◻	167	Yellow-beige
1096	╱	168	Pewter
9046	✕	321	Christmas red
211	◆	505	Jade green
874	⧄	676	Old gold
239	◯	702	Christmas green
256	△	704	Chartreuse
295	▢	726	Light topaz
306	☆	728	Topaz
380	◆	779	Cocoa
882	▭	945	Ivory
382	■	3371	Black-brown
904	#	3787	Brown-gray
	✳	002	Kreinik Gold #4 very fine braid (1X)

BLENDED NEEDLE CROSS-STITCH

ANCHOR		DMC	
002	•	000	White (1X) and
		100	Kreinik White blending filament (4X)
939	◺	156	Lavender-blue (1X) and
		025	Kreinik Grey blending filament (4X)
9046	◉	321	Christmas red (1X) and
		003	Kreinik Red blending filament (4X)
038	▶	335	Rose (1X) and
		031	Kreinik Crimson blending filament (4X)

BLENDED NEEDLE CROSS-STITCH

ANCHOR		DMC	
239	◐	702	Christmas green (1X) and
		008	Kreinik Green blending filament (4X)
256	⊞	704	Chartreuse (1X) and
		015	Kreinik Chartreuse blending filament (4X)
295	▽	726	Light topaz (1X) and
		091	Kreinik Star yellow blending filament (4X)
306	⊕	728	Topaz (1X) and
		127	Kreinik Yellow-orange blending filament (4X)
137	◀	798	Delft blue (1X) and
		051HL	Kreinik Sapphire Hi Lustre blending filament (4X)

BACKSTITCH

ANCHOR		DMC	
1094	╱	151	Dusty rose – lamb nose (1X)
280	╱	166	Moss green – holly leaves (1X)
211	╱	505	Jade green – holly leaves, saddle and wagon (1X)
306	╱	728	Topaz – dove legs (2X)
065	╱	777	Raspberry – horse, nutcracker, "Joy" (1X); and lettering (2X)
	╱	002	Kreinik Gold #4 very fine braid – soldier's hat, horse mane and tail, saddle detail, rocker, and train window (1X)
382	╱	3371	Black-brown – all other stitches (1X); holly and cat whiskers (2X)

STRAIGHT STITCH (2X)

ANCHOR		DMC	
239	╱	702	Christmas green – evergreen branch in middle train car, in dove's beak, and by horse

TASSEL

9046	✕	321	Christmas red tassel wrapped with
		002	Kreinik gold #4 very fine braid – small tassels on horse

MILL HILL BEAD

●	03040	Flat black antique seed bead – eyes of soldier, horse, dove, nutcracker, cat sheep, and dog
●	03049	Rich red antique seed bead – trees by name, and ornament in train car
○	00557	Gold seed bead – tree tops by name, soldier's buttons, horse's bridle, saddle and rocker, nutcracker's hat, train engine
◯	13018	Light Colorado topaz Crystal Treasures round bead – name
●	13022	Siam AB Crystal Treasures round bead – poinsettia leaf in train car and by horse
◇	03049	Rich red antique seed bead and
	72052	Red velvet small bugle bead – bows on cat, sheep, dog and horn

ATTACHMENT

⊗		¼" yellow button attached with
	40557	Mill Hill gold petite glass seed bead – middle train car and caboose
⊗		⅝" red button attached with
	00557	Mill Hill gold glass seed bead – train engine
⊗		1" red button attached with
	00557	Mill Hill gold glass seed beads – train engine

Stitch count: *176 high x 132 wide*

Finished design size:
14-count fabric – 12½ x 9½ inches

Christmas Joy Pillow

Supplies
- 12×12½" piece of 32-count antique ivory Belfast linen
- Cotton embroidery floss
- Kreinik blending filament
- Mill Hill petite seed beads
- ⅓ yard of coral print fabric
- 1⅓ yards of light-gold sew-in twisted cording
- Matching sewing thread
- Polyester fiberfill

Stitches
Center and stitch the chart on linen. Use two plies of floss to work the stitches over two threads of the fabric unless otherwise specified. Attach the seed beads using one ply of matching floss. Press the stitched piece from the back.

Assembly
Center the design and trim the stitched piece to a 7¾×8" rectangle. From coral print fabric, cut two 2⅝×8" side sashing strips, two 2⅝×11" top and bottom sashing strips, and an 11×11¼" backing. Measurements include a ½" seam allowance.

Right sides together, sew short sashing strips to each side of the stitched piece. Press seam allowances toward the sashing strips. Sew long sashing strips to the top and bottom of the stitched piece. Press.

Using a zipper foot, baste the twisted cording to the perimeter of the pillow front. Right sides together and using a zipper foot, sew the pillow front to the back along the basting lines, leaving an opening along the bottom for turning and stuffing. Trim the seams. Turn the pillow right side out and press. Stuff the pillow with fiberfill. Slip-stitch the opening closed.

Christmas Joy Ornaments

Supplies for each ornament
- 8" square of 28-count Waterlily Jobelan fabric or 28-count Appleblossom linen
- Cotton embroidery floss
- Kreinik blending filament
- Mill Hill petite seed beads
- 3" square of coordinating cotton fabric
- 7" length of ⅛"-wide ribbon or fine gold cording
- Matching sewing thread
- Polyester fiberfill

Stitches
Center and stitch the desired motif from the Christmas Joy Pillow chart, *pages 70–71,* on the fabric. Use two plies of floss to work the stitches over two threads of the fabric unless otherwise specified. Attach the seed beads using one ply of matching floss. Press the stitched piece from the back.

Assembly
Center the design and trim the stitched piece to 3" square. For the hanging loop, fold the ribbon or cording in half. Sew the ribbon ends to the center top of the stitched piece.

Right sides together, sew the ornament front to the back with a ¼" seam allowance, leaving an opening along the bottom for turning and stuffing. Trim the corners. Turn the ornament right side out and press. Stuff with polyester fiberfill. Slip-stitch the opening closed.

Christmas Joy Pillow and Ornaments Key

CROSS-STITCH (2X)

ANCHOR		DMC	
002	•	000	White
001	◇	B5200	Bright white
1025	✕	347	Deep salmon
362	▽	437	Medium tan
878	▲	501	Dark blue-green
875	⊙	503	True blue-green
1041	◉	535	Ash gray
392	✛	642	Medium beige-gray
874	✳	676	Light old gold
885	☆	677	Pale old gold
887		739	Pale tan
234	╱	762	Pearl gray
337	◩	922	Copper
1012	–	948	Peach
1023	⌃	3712	Medium salmon
868	⌐	3779	Terra-cotta
1088	✚	3790	Deep beige-gray
877	◆	3815	Dark celadon green
876	▦	3816	True celadon green

BACKSTITCH (1X)

1025	╱	347	Deep salmon – outline inside the checked border, and "Christmas JOY"
878	╱	501	Dark blue-green – dashed border around each motif, "Ho!Ho!Ho!", "Noel" on stocking, leaves of flowers on heart
1088	╱	3790	Deep beige-gray – wreath, gingerbread man, chimney and above the door and door window on house, and Christmas tree
1041	╱	535	Ash gray – all other stitches

FRENCH KNOT (2X wrapped twice)

1025	●	347	Deep salmon – heart, "i" in Christmas
878	●	501	Dark blue-green – exclamation points on Ho! Ho! Ho!
1088	●	3790	Deep beige-gray – gingerbread man's eyes, and snowman's eyes

ZIGZAG STITCH (2X)

878	∧∧	501	Dark blue-green – zigzag between each motif and on stocking

BLENDED NEEDLE SMYRNA CROSS-STITCH

874	✳	676	Light old gold (1X) and
		002HL	Kreinik Gold Hi Lustre blending filament (1X) – border around wreath

BLENDED NEEDLE STAR STITCH

874	✳	676	Light old gold (1X) and
		002HL	Kreinik Gold Hi Lustre blending filament (1X) – backgrounds of center square and bottom right square

MILL HILL PETITE GLASS SEED BEAD

○	40557	Gold – tree

Sampler stitch count:
101 high x 101 wide

Sampler finished design size:
32-count fabric – 6¼ x 6¼ inches

Ornaments stitch count:
29 high x 29 wide

Ornaments finished design size:
28-count fabric – 2 x 2 inches

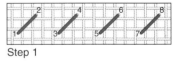

Smyrna-Cross Stitch

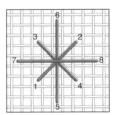

Star Stitch

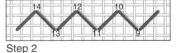

Step 1

Step 2

Zigzag Stitch

Holiday Pocket Ornaments

Mitten Pocket Ornament

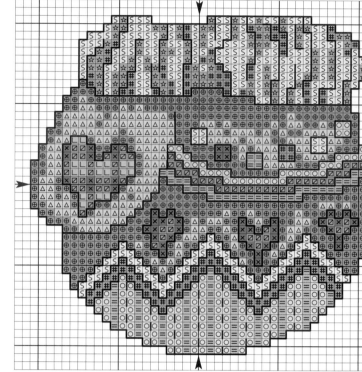

Holiday Pocket Ornaments

Supplies for each ornament
- 8" square of 14-count white Aida cloth
- Cotton embroidery floss
- 4" square of white felt
- 8" length of ⅛"-wide red satin ribbon
- Fray Check liquid plastic

Stitches
Center and stitch the desired chart on the Aida cloth. Use two plies of floss to work the stitches over one square of the fabric unless otherwise specified. Press the stitched piece from the back.

Assembly
Trim the stitched piece two squares beyond the stitches on the sides and bottom of the design and one square beyond the stitches on the top. To prevent raveling, apply Fray Check to the edges of the trimmed stitched piece. Let the Fray Check dry.

Center the stitched piece on white felt. Use one ply of white floss to backstitch the stitched piece to the felt along the side and bottom edges, 1 square beyond the design. Leave top open. Trim the felt close to the stitched piece.

For the hanging loop, use a needle to thread the ribbon ends through the felt; knot each ribbon end.

Santa Pocket Ornament

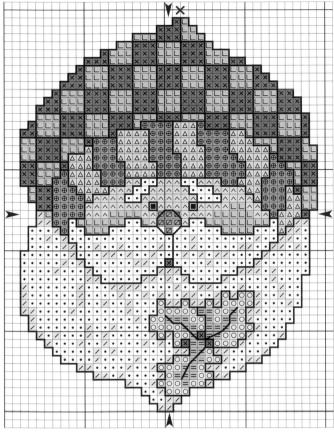

Snowman Pocket Ornament

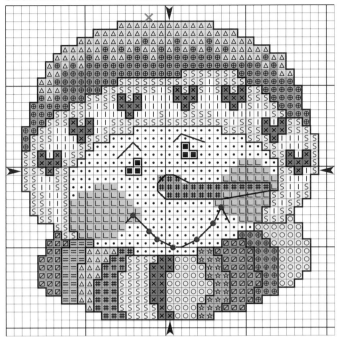

Holiday Pocket Ornaments

CROSS-STITCH (2X)

ANCHOR		DMC	
002	•	000	White
235	/	318	Steel
046	✕	666	Red
227	═	701	Christmas green
257	O	703	Chartreuse
305	S	725	Topaz
300	I	745	Yellow
868	∧	754	Peach
1022	L	760	Salmon

CROSS-STITCH (2X)

ANCHOR		DMC	
307	☆	783	Christmas gold
140	△	813	Powder blue
161	⊕	826	Bright blue
381	■	938	Coffee brown
035	▨	3705	Watermelon
324	⧈	3853	Autumn gold

BACKSTITCH (1X)

381	/	938	Coffee brown – all stitches (1X)

RUNNING STITCH (1X)

ANCHOR		DMC	
046	/	666	Red – fingertip of mitten (2X)

FRENCH KNOT (3X wrapped once)

381	●	938	Coffee brown – snowman's mouth

TASSEL

046	✕	666	Red – top of Santa's hat
305	✕	725	Topaz – top of snowman's hat

Mitten stitch count: *42 high x 42 wide*
Mitten finished design size:
14-count fabric – 3 x 3 inches
Santa stitch count: *49 high x 37 wide*
Santa finished design size:
14-count fabric – 3¹/₂ x 2²/₃ inches
Snowman stitch count: *37 high x 37 wide*
Snowman finished design size:
14-count fabric – 2²/₃ x 2²/₃ inches

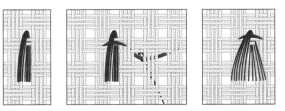

Holiday Pocket Ornaments Tassel Diagrams

Happy Holiday Home

Dress your house in festive Christmas finery.

Mention yuletide decorating, and cross-stitchers' fingers just get happy—whether it's December 26 or the middle of July. Crafters always are on the lookout for something new and pretty to make and add to their homes during the Christmas season. Get ready with your needles and thread: this selection of stitchery projects overflows with ideas you'll want to start on right away. Choose a nostalgic cookie tray, a parade of snowmen mantel decoration, elegant hand towels, or even stitched greeting cards. There's something to fill every room of your house with joy!

Scatter fresh blooms in your holiday home with cross-stitched towels. These beribboned poinsettia designs suit every room of the house. Stitch them on specialty towels with Aida inserts, or on the corners of tablecloths or place mats. You can even work several on perforated paper for tree trims.

Project instructions begin on page 90.
Designs: Julia Lucas.

Pack a mantel with personality when you display this cheery greeting. You'll have

fun stitching every grin as you watch each snow friend come to life. Work each figure on Aida

and adhere it to a stiffened-felt backing with a loop of ribbon.

Project instructions begin on page 83. Design: Ursula Michael.

Some Christmas greetings are special beyond words. To send cards with a handcrafted touch, try these quick-stitch holiday tree motifs. Your friends will appreciate their messages of love and joy, and the stitchery is pretty enough to frame for next year's decorating. (You even could make a gift of a frame to fit around the already matted design.)

Project instructions begin on page 92.
Design: Cathy Ritchie.

Wrap a foam wreath with yards of beautiful ribbons. Use wire-edge ribbon topped with ready-to-stitch Aida banding, embellished with holly clusters and "Joy" from the stitched greeting card, *opposite*.

Project instructions begin on page 94.
Design: Cathy Ritchie.

A beautiful stitched Christmas card receives high status during the season and is treasured for years to come. Create an heirloom greeting set off by elegant paper. Or make the stitchery easily detachable so it can be framed or used as a tree ornament.

Project instructions begin on page 94. Design: Cathy Ritchie.

A triple treat? Yes! This delectable treasure of cross–stitch and counted embroidery displays a tasty batch of Christmas goodies on a practical serving tray. Protected beneath glass, the evenweave recipe will never become dog-eared or stained. Finish your stitchery with a conventional frame if you prefer. Either way, it's so pretty you'll want to keep it on display all season long.

Project instructions begin on page 87.
Design: Gail Bussi.

Set the stage for warm holiday welcome at your front door. A nutcracker soldier stands sentinel as a decorative bellpull, greeting every passerby. Bright letters, stacked one upon the other, stretch along the length of linen for an elegant Christmas keepsake.

Project instructions begin on page 96. Design: Mike Vickery.

Quick-Stitch Snowmen Ornaments

Supplies for one ornament

- 8" square of 14-count blue butterfly Aida cloth
- Cotton embroidery floss
- Mill Hill petite seed beads for the baby
- Just Another Button Co.'s small cardinal, solid red heart, candy cane, small red peppermint, blue mitten, and snowflake buttons (optional)
- Stiffened felt: 3⅝×4" rectangle of white and 3⅛×3½" rectangle of blue, green, or red
- 6" length of ⅛"-wide blue, green, or red satin ribbon
- Pinking shears; thick white crafts glue

Stitches

Center and stitch snowmen from the chart on Aida cloth. Use three plies of floss to work stitches over one square of fabric unless otherwise specified. Attach

petite seed beads with one ply of matching floss for the baby's eyes. Press the stitched piece from the back. Use matching floss to sew on the buttons.

Assembly

Trim the stitched piece to 2⅝×3". Center the stitched piece on blue, green, or red felt trimmed with pinking shears. Glue in place. For the hanging loop, glue ends of matching ribbon to the top center back of the colored felt. Center and glue the colored felt on the white felt.

Quick-Stitch Snowman Framed Piece

Supplies

- 8" square of 16-count white Aida cloth
- Cotton embroidery floss
- Desired frame

Stitches

Center and stitch a snowman from the Quick-Stitch Snowmen chart, *pages 84–86,* on Aida cloth. Use two plies of

floss to work the stitches over one square of fabric unless otherwise specified. If you like, omit the initial. Press the stitched piece from the back. Frame as desired.

Snowman M #1

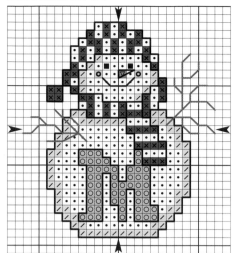

Stitch count: *27 high x 24 wide*
Finished design size:
14-count fabric – 2 x 1³/₄ inches

Snowman R #1

Stitch count: *28 high x 24 wide*
Finished design size:
14-count fabric – 2 x 1³/₄ inches

Snowman Y

Stitch count: *29 high x 25 wide*
Finished design size:
14-count fabric – 2¹/₈ x 1⁷/₈ inches

Snowman E

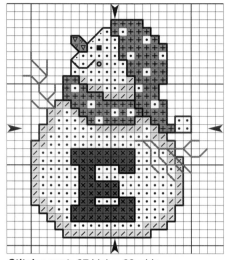

Stitch count: *27 high x 23 wide*
Finished design size:
14-count fabric – 2 x 1²/₃ inches

Snowman R#2

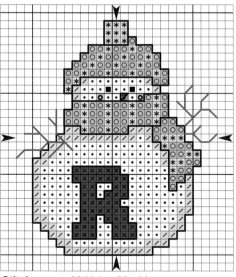

Stitch count: *29 high x 25 wide*
Finished design size:
14-count fabric – 2¹/₈ x 1⁷/₈ inches

Snowman C

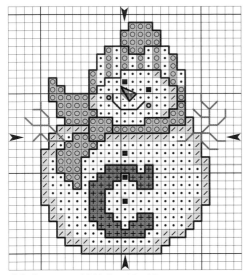

Stitch count: 29 high x 25 wide
Finished design size:
14-count fabric – 2⅛ x 1⅞ inches

Snowman I

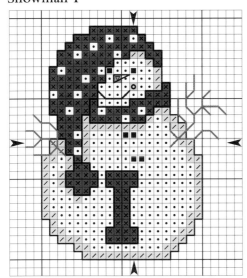

Stitch count: 29 high x 25 wide
Finished design size:
14-count fabric – 2⅛ x 1⅞ inches

Snowman S

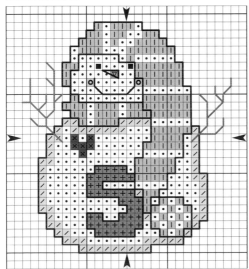

Stitch count: 29 high x 26 wide
Finished design size:
14-count fabric – 2⅛ x 1⅞ inches

Quick-Stitch Snowmen

Snowman H

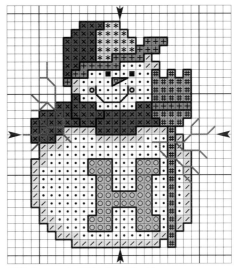

Stitch count: 28 high x 24 wide
Finished design size:
14-count fabric – 2 x 1¾ inches

Quick-Stitch Snowmen Key

CROSS-STITCH (3X)

ANCHOR		DMC
002	⊡	000 White
403	■	310 Black
9046	✕	321 Christmas red
9575	◎	353 Peach
362	⊞	437 Tan
332	▽	608 Orange
239	○	702 Christmas green
305	✱	725 Topaz
137	✛	798 Delft blue
158	╱	828 Powder blue
042	⊥	961 Rose-pink

BACKSTITCH (1X)

8581	╱	646 Beaver gray – arms (2X)
403	╱	310 Black – all other stitches (1X)

Quick-Stitch Snowmen

Snowman T

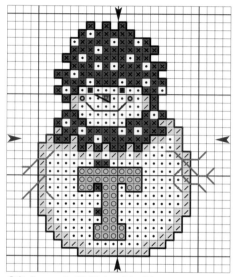

Stitch count: *29 high x 24 wide*
Finished design size:
14-count fabric – 2⅛ x 1¾ inches

Snowman A

Stitch count: *29 high x 27 wide*
Finished design size:
14-count fabric – 2⅛ x 2 inches

Snowman M #2

Stitch count: *30 high x 21 wide*
Finished design size:
14-count fabric – 2⅛ x 1½ inches

Quick-Stitch Snowmen Key

CROSS-STITCH (3X)

ANCHOR		DMC
002	·	000 White
403	■	310 Black
9046	✕	321 Christmas red
9575	⊙	353 Peach
362	⌗	437 Tan
332	▽	608 Orange
239	◎	702 Christmas green
305	✳	725 Topaz
137	＋	798 Delft blue
158	╱	828 Powder blue
042	▯	961 Rose-pink

BACKSTITCH (1X)

8581	╱	646 Beaver gray – arms (2X)
403	╱	310 Black – all other stitches (1X)

MILL HILL SEED BEAD

42014 Black – baby's eyes on snowman "M" #2

The chart and key are on pages 88–89.

Christmas Kitchen

Supplies
- 17×14½" piece of 26-count golden flax linen
- Cotton embroidery floss
- 16½×12½" tray with a 12×9" design area
- 16½×12½" rectangle of fleece
- Spray adhesive
- Thick white crafts glue or tape

Stitches
Center and stitch the chart on linen. Use two plies of floss to work stitches over two threads of fabric. Press from back.

Assembly
Remove the mounting board from the tray, and lightly spray it with adhesive.

Position the fleece on the board; trim it to the size of the board. Center the stitched piece face-up on the fleece-covered board; glue or tape it in place. Insert the mounted stitchery according to the tray manufacturer's instructions.

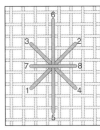

Star Stitch

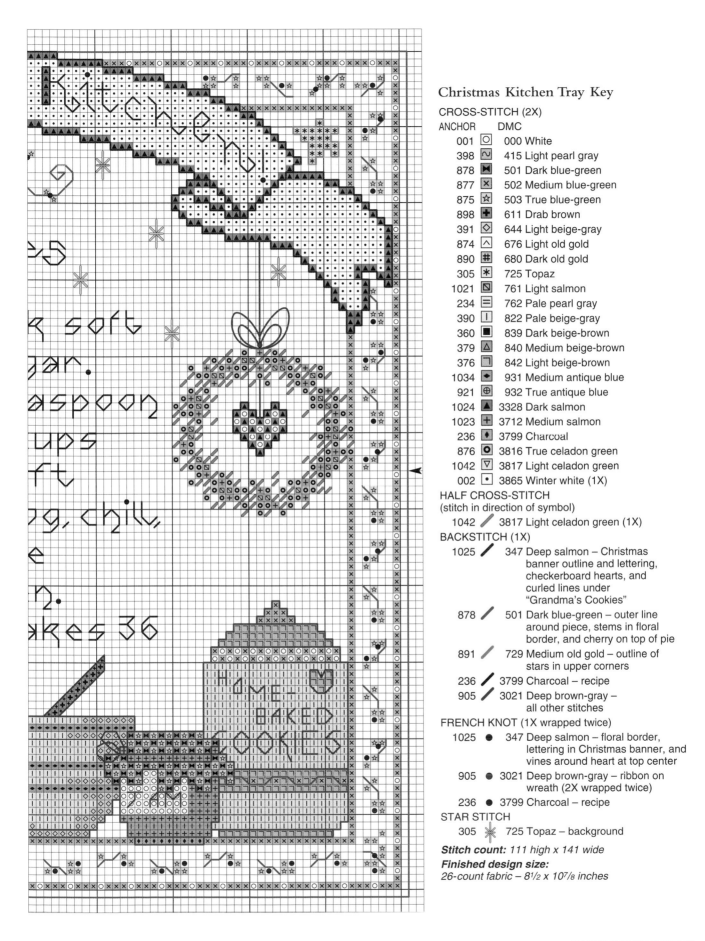

Christmas Kitchen Tray Key

CROSS-STITCH (2X)

ANCHOR		DMC	
001	○	000	White
398	~	415	Light pearl gray
878	◙	501	Dark blue-green
877	✕	502	Medium blue-green
875	☆	503	True blue-green
898	✚	611	Drab brown
391	◇	644	Light beige-gray
874	∧	676	Light old gold
890	⊞	680	Dark old gold
305	✳	725	Topaz
1021	⊠	761	Light salmon
234	⊟	762	Pale pearl gray
390	▯	822	Pale beige-gray
360	■	839	Dark beige-brown
379	△	840	Medium beige-brown
376	⊐	842	Light beige-brown
1034	◆	931	Medium antique blue
921	⊕	932	True antique blue
1024	▲	3328	Dark salmon
1023	✢	3712	Medium salmon
236	◈	3799	Charcoal
876	◎	3816	True celadon green
1042	▽	3817	Light celadon green
002	·	3865	Winter white (1X)

HALF CROSS-STITCH
(stitch in direction of symbol)

1042	╱	3817	Light celadon green (1X)

BACKSTITCH (1X)

1025	╱	347	Deep salmon – Christmas banner outline and lettering, checkerboard hearts, and curled lines under "Grandma's Cookies"
878	╱	501	Dark blue-green – outer line around piece, stems in floral border, and cherry on top of pie
891	╱	729	Medium old gold – outline of stars in upper corners
236	╱	3799	Charcoal – recipe
905	╱	3021	Deep brown-gray – all other stitches

FRENCH KNOT (1X wrapped twice)

1025	●	347	Deep salmon – floral border, lettering in Christmas banner, and vines around heart at top center
905	●	3021	Deep brown-gray – ribbon on wreath (2X wrapped twice)
236	●	3799	Charcoal – recipe

STAR STITCH

305	✳	725	Topaz – background

Stitch count: *111 high x 141 wide*

Finished design size:
26-count fabric – 8¹⁄₂ x 10⁷⁄₈ inches

Love and Joy Towels

Love Towel

Love and Joy Towels

Supplies
- Purchased 15×25" white huck towel with a 4½×5¾" 14-count Aida-cloth insert
- Cotton embroidery floss
- Kreinik fine braid

Stitches
Center and stitch the desired chart on the Aida-cloth towel insert. Use three plies of floss to work stitches over one square of fabric unless otherwise specified. Press the finished towel from the back.

Joy Towel

Love and Joy Towels Key

CROSS-STITCH (3X)

ANCHOR		DMC
1006	☒	304 Christmas red
218	◗	319 Dark pistachio
215	▽	320 True pistachio
217	+	367 Medium pistachio
045	▲	814 Dark garnet
1005	#	816 Light garnet
305	／	3821 Straw
019	○	3831 Raspberry

BACKSTITCH (1X)

ANCHOR		DMC
218	／	319 Dark pistachio – lettering
045	／	814 Dark garnet – small poinsettia on ribbon
	／	002HL Kreinik Gold hi-lustre #8 fine braid – poinsettias and ribbon

Love Towel stitch count:
75 high x 57 wide

Love Towel finished design size:
14-count fabric – 5³⁄₈ x 4 inches

Joy Towel stitch count:
75 high x 55 wide

Joy Towel finished design sizes:
14-count fabric – 5³⁄₈ x 4 inches

Christmas Greeting Cards

with interfacing. For the card, fold red cardstock in half to make a 4½×6½" rectangle. Use the crafts knife to cut a 3⅛" square opening in green cardstock. Center the stitchery in the opening and tape it to the back of the green cardstock. Mount the green cardstock on the front of the red card with double-stick tape.

Tree Greeting Card

Supplies
- 8" square of 18-count Williamsburg blue Aida cloth
- Cotton embroidery floss
- Kreinik blending filament
- 3½" square of fusible interfacing
- 4×8" piece of blue cardstock
- 3¾" square of white cardstock
- Crafts knife
- Double-stick tape

Stitches
Center and stitch the chart on the Aida cloth. Use one ply of floss to work the stitches over one square of the fabric unless otherwise specified. Press the stitched piece from the back.

Assembly
Center and fuse the interfacing to the back of the stitched piece, following interfacing manufacturer's instructions. Trim the stitched piece edges even with interfacing.

For the card, fold blue cardstock in half to make a 4" square. Cut a 3" square opening in the front of the card. Center and cut a 2⅝" square opening on the white cardstock. Center and mount the white cardstock on the inside front of the card. Center the stitchery in the opening and tape it to the white cardstock.

Noel Greeting Card

Supplies
- 9" square of 18-count white Aida cloth
- Cotton embroidery floss
- Kreinik blending filament
- 3½" square of fusible interfacing
- 6½×9" rectangle of red cardstock
- 4×6" rectangle of green cardstock
- Crafts knife
- Double-stick tape

Stitches
Center and stitch the chart on the Aida cloth. Use one ply of floss to work stitches over one square of fabric unless otherwise specified. Press the stitched piece from the back side.

Assembly
Center and fuse the interfacing to the back of the stitched piece, following interfacing manufacturer's instructions. Trim the stitched piece edges even

Noel Greeting Card

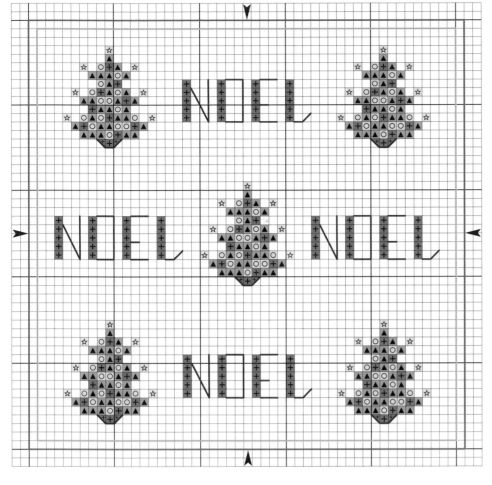

Noel Greeting Card Key

CROSS-STITCH (1X)

ANCHOR		DMC	
1006	+	304	Christmas red
683	▲	500	Deep blue-green
877	○	502	Medium blue-green
	☆	001	Kreinik silver blending filament

BACKSTITCH (1X)

1006	/	304	Christmas red – lettering, tree base
683	/	500	Deep blue-green – outer border
877	/	502	Medium blue-green – inner border

Stitch count: *50 high x 51 wide*
Finished design sizes:
18-count fabric – 2¾ x 2¾ inches

Tree Greeting Card

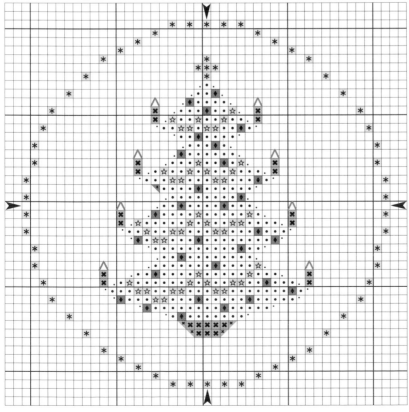

Tree Greeting Card Key

CROSS-STITCH (1X)

ANCHOR		DMC	
002	•	000	White
979	✖	312	Navy
	☆	001	Kreinik silver blending filament
	✱	002	Kreinik gold blending filament

BLENDED-NEEDLE CROSS-STITCH (2X)

979	◆	312	Navy (1X) and 002 Kreinik gold blending filament (1X)

STRAIGHT STITCH (1X)

	/	002	Kreinik gold blending filament – candle flames

Stitch count: *43 high x 43 wide*
Finished design sizes:
18-count fabric – 2⅜ x 2⅜ inches

Joy to the World Card and Wreath Banding

over one square of the fabric unless otherwise specified. Press the stitched piece from the back.

Assembly

Wrap ivory ribbon around the wreath, overlapping edges to completely cover the wreath. Use straight pins to secure the ends. Wrap the metallic gold-and-sheer ribbon over the ivory ribbon. Wrap the banding around the wreath with the wraps about 2½" apart. Secure greenery and berries to the wreath at the center bottom with florist's picks. Tie a bow using the metallic gold ribbon and florist's wire. Use the wire to attach the bow to wreath and to form a hanging loop at the back center top.

Joy to the World Card

Supplies
- 9" square of 18-count white Aida cloth
- Cotton embroidery floss
- 5" square of fusible interfacing
- 7¾×11½" rectangle of white cardstock
- 5½" square of red cardstock
- Double-stick tape

Stitches

Center and stitch the chart on the Aida cloth. Use one ply of floss to work the stitches over one square of the fabric unless otherwise specified. Press piece from back.

Assembly

Center and fuse the interfacing to the back of the stitched piece, following interfacing manufacturer's instructions. Trim stitched piece edges even with interfacing.

For the card, fold the white cardstock in half to make a 5¾×7¾" rectangle. Cut a 4"-diameter circle opening in the front of the card. Cut a 3⅞"-diameter circle

opening centered on red cardstock. Center and mount red cardstock on the inside front of the card using double-stick tape. Center stitchery in the opening and tape it to the red cardstock.

Joy Wreath Banding

Supplies
- 65" length of 1¼"-wide 16-count red-and-white Aida-cloth banding
- Cotton embroidery floss
- 12"-diameter straw wreath
- 5½ yards of 2"-wide ivory ribbon
- 5½ yards of 2¼"-wide metallic gold-and-sheer ribbon
- 2 yards of 1½"-wide metallic gold ribbon
- Straight pins
- Artificial greenery and berries
- Florist's picks and wire

Stitches

Center and stitch alternating holly and Joy motifs from the Joy to the World Band chart, *opposite,* on the banding, leaving two squares between motifs. Use two plies of floss to work the stitches

Joy to the World Card and Wreath Banding Key

CROSS-STITCH (2X)

ANCHOR		DMC	
9046	☒	321	Christmas red
683	▲	500	Deep blue-green
878	⊞	501	Dark blue-green
877	⊙	502	Medium blue-green

BACKSTITCH (1X)

9046	╱	321	Christmas red – berries, lettering

Card stitch count: 64 high x 64 wide
Card finished design sizes:
18-count fabric – 3½ x 3½ inches
Banding stitch count (one repeat):
14 high x 77 wide
Banding finished design size:
14-count fabric – 1 x 5½ inches

Joy to the World Card

Joy Wreath Banding

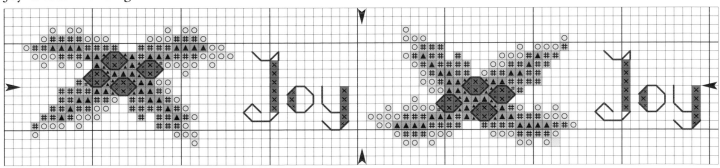

A Season of Sharing

Great ideas for gift giving will be appreciated by all this holiday season.

When it comes to giving, everyone knows it's the thought that counts. When you spend time cross-stitching just the right gift for a good friend or close relative, you can be sure that your efforts are appreciated. The original holiday designs on the following pages will keep you busy stitching pretty and useful presents for family, neighbors, teachers, coworkers, and everyone on your gift list. Your thoughtful gestures will have your loved ones singing your praises not only at Christmas, but for many years to come.

Try topping these! Tiny jars become welcome Christmas gifts when they're capped in cheery cross-stitches and beads. Stitched with embroidery floss over easy-on-the-eyes Aida cloth, these rosy-cheeked Santas cover lids with bright smiles amid three dimensional colors.

Project instructions begin on page 113. Design: Ursula Michael.

Do you know someone who leaps for that first cup of morning coffee? Hand him or her this stitch-and-mortar cottage! Ready to hug a favorite mug, it also can double as a gift wrap when you tuck a new mug, espresso beans, or bag of cocoa under the roof.

Project instructions begin on page 108.
Design: Patricia Andrle.

What could be sweeter than three little bears on a baby bib? Welcome a new arrival with your own cross-stitched creation, or make several to give as gifts. The bib, ready-made with an Aida band insert, takes on personality when you add one, two, or three darling sweatered teddy bears.

Project instructions begin on page 112.
Design: Barbara Sestok.

Good things do indeed come in small packages. The little gems on these two pages each measure about 1×1½" and include meticulous basket-weave stitches that cover their entire backgrounds. Set into tiny jewelry frames, the designs can be used for many gift and decorating ideas. Thread a soft ribbon through the loop on the frame of this twinkling design to make a pretty necklace.

Project instructions begin on page 116.
Design: Linda Stoltz.

This petite folk-art heart treasure says "I love you." Worked on 40-count silk linen, the hundreds of tiny half-crosses create art in miniature. Present this loving memento tied to a bright holiday bauble.

Project instructions begin on page 117.
Design: Linda Stoltz.

A downpour of tiny stitches fills every inch of this delightful charm. If you plan to make several, consider shortcuts. Work your designs on colored canvas and leave backgrounds unstitched. Tie charms to stemware for party favors or use them to personalize packages.

Project instructions begin on page 115. Design: Linda Stoltz.

Pillow-top greetings fit into a basket of goodies or rest on a mantel to remind recipients of your wishes for a home full of holiday cheer. Quickly stitched, layered, and embellished with a wooden snowman and ribbon bow, this small gift carries with it big sentiment.

Project instructions begin on page 110. Design: Lizzie Kate.

Our homey pillow design does double duty as a tiny ornament. This simpler version focuses on the house, stitched on wintry powder blue Aida. Scent it to use in dresser drawers, or slip it over a doorknob to add a reminder of Christmas all around the house.

Project instructions begin on page 110. Design: Lizzie Kate.

Win a Santa lover's heart with this whimsical version of the jolly old elf. Donning festive winter wear, this St. Nick stitches up quick as a wink. With specialty-stitch buttons, a merry message, and primitive stars dancing beside him, this Santa will be cherished by all ages.

Project instructions begin on page 118. Design: Cecelia Turner.

The fragrances of the season evoke memories of Christmases past.

Brighten a mantel or kitchen counter during dreary winter weeks with this colorful

still life inserted into a serving tray.

Project instructions begin on page 120. Design: Barbara Sestok from illustrations by Annie Lang.

Christmas Cottage Mug Cozy

Christmas Cottage Mug Cozy—Front and Back

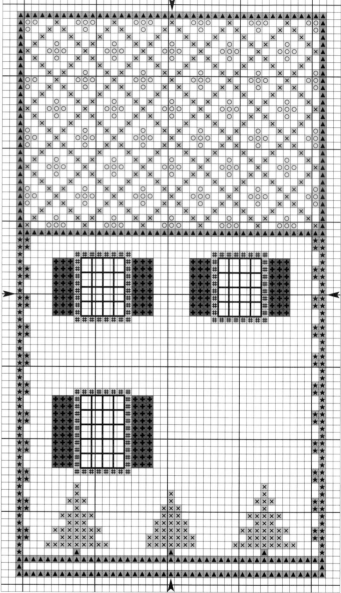

Cottage Mug Cozy

Supplies

- 20-count bone Lugana fabric: 2—10×13" rectangles for the front and back and 2—10×12" rectangles for the sides
- #5 pearl cotton
- Cotton embroidery floss
- ¼ yard of fleece
- ¼ yard of red-print cotton fabric
- Sewing thread: dark green, dark gray, and red
- Mill Hill buttons

Stitches

Center and stitch each chart on the appropriate piece of fabric. Use one strand of pearl cotton to work the stitches over two threads of the fabric unless otherwise specified. Press the stitched pieces from the back sides.

Assembly

Trim the stitched pieces ½" beyond the stitched area of each design. Use each trimmed stitched piece as a pattern to cut one fleece interlining and one red-print fabric lining.

Christmas Cottage Mug Cozy—Sides

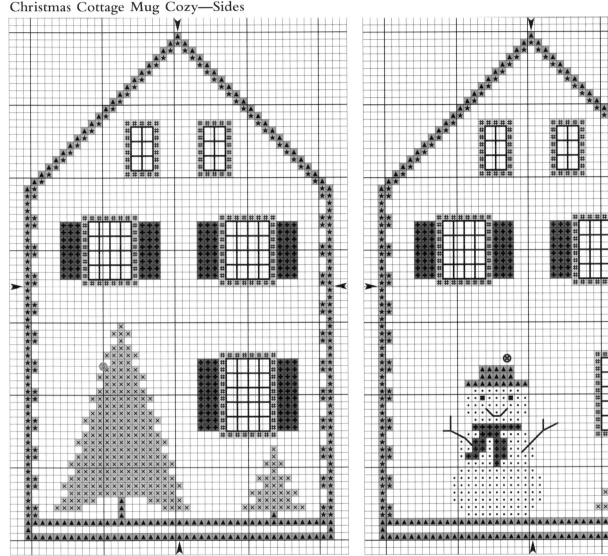

Baste fleece to the wrong side of each stitched piece using a ½" seam allowance. Right sides together, sew each stitched piece to lining along the basting lines, leaving an opening on one side edge for turning. Trim the seams and turn right side out. Press. Slip-stitch the openings closed.

Use matching sewing thread to blindstitch the top edges of the cozy front and back together. Blindstitch the cozy sides to the front and back. Sew the buttons on with red sewing thread, referring to the charts for placement.

Christmas Cottage Mug Cozy Key

CROSS-STITCH (1X)

ANCHOR		DMC	
002	·	000	White #5 pearl cotton
403	■	310	Black #5 pearl cotton
235	⊞	318	Light steel #5 pearl cotton
218	▲	319	Dark pistachio #5 pearl cotton
215	✕	320	True pistachio #5 pearl cotton
214	○	368	Light pistachio #5 pearl cotton
400	★	414	Dark steel #5 pearl cotton
043	✚	815	Garnet #5 pearl cotton

BACKSTITCH (1X)

403	╱	310 Black cotton floss – all stitches

MILL HILL BUTTONS

⊗ 86150 Wreath
⊗ 86230 Cardinal (left)
⊗ 86231 Cardinal (right)

COTTAGE FRONT AND BACK
Stitch count: 78 high x 43 wide

Finished design size:
20-count fabric – 7³⁄₄ x 4¹⁄₃ inches

COTTAGE SIDES
Stitch count: 70 high x 43 wide

Finished design size:
20-count fabric – 7 x 4¹⁄₃ inches

Happy Holidays Pillow and House Ornament

(DMC 500) floss. Combine the cut lengths into a single strand. Secure one end of the strands and tightly wind to twist. Hold the ends, fold the strand in half, and let the halves twist around each other. Knot both ends to secure. Beginning and ending at the top right corner of the stitched piece, hand-sew the twisted cording to the pillow front along the outer edges of the stitched piece. Knot the twisted cording at the corner, and trim the excess.

Turn back the top right corner of the pillow front; tack in place. Tie a sheer ribbon into a bow. Center the bow on the folded corner. Stitch in place with a snowman button.

House Ornament

Supplies

- 9×10" piece of 14-count blue butterfly Aida cloth
- Cotton embroidery floss
- Mill Hill Glass Treasures: Evergreen
- 4×4½" rectangle of self-stick mounting board with foam
- Thick white crafts glue
- 18" length of ½"-wide dark green braid
- 9" length of ⅜"-wide dark green ribbon
- 3½×4" rectangle of white felt

Stitches

Center and stitch the house motif from the Happy Holidays chart, *opposite,* on the Aida cloth. Use two plies of floss to work the stitches over one square of the fabric unless otherwise specified. Press the stitched piece from the back. Sew the evergreen on with two plies of matching floss, referring to the photograph for placement.

Assembly

Peel the protective paper from the mounting board. Center the foam side on the back of the stitched piece: press to stick. Trim the excess fabric 2" beyond the edges of the board. Fold the edges of the fabric to the back, and glue in place.

Glue the braid to the edges of the ornament, folding the ends under. Glue the ribbon ends to the top back corners. Glue the felt to the back.

Happy Holidays Pillow

Supplies

- 10×9" rectangle of 32-count moss green linen
- Cotton embroidery floss, including an extra skein of garnet and blue-green for the twisted cording
- ½" heart charm
- ⅓ yard of green-print cotton fabric
- ⅓ yard of red-print cotton fabric
- Matching sewing thread
- Polyester fiberfill
- 12" length of 1"-wide green sheer ribbon
- Mill Hill snowman button

Stitches

Find the center of the chart and center of the linen to begin stitching. Use two plies of floss to work the stitches over two threads of the fabric unless otherwise specified. Attach the charm with two plies of matching floss. Press the stitched piece from the back.

Assembly

Center the design and trim the stitched piece to 6¼×5¾". From green fabric, cut a 9¼×8¾" backing piece, two 2×5¾" sashing strips, and two 2×9¼" sashing strips. From red fabric, cut two 9¼×8¾" lining pieces. All measurements include a ¼" seam allowance unless otherwise specified.

Right sides together, sew the 2×5¾" strips to the sides; press seams toward sashing. Sew the 2×9¼" sashing strips to the top and bottom. Press.

Right sides together, sew the pieced front to a 9¼×8¾" red lining, leaving an opening on the bottom edge for turning. Trim the seams. Turn the pillow front right side out and press. Slip-stitch the opening closed.

Right sides together, sew the green back to a red lining, leaving an opening on the bottom edge for turning. Trim the seams. Turn the pillow back right side out and press. Slip-stitch the opening closed.

To assemble the pillow, center the front on the back, lining sides together. Sew all the layers together along the outer edges of the stitched piece, leaving an opening at the center bottom for stuffing. Firmly stuff the pillow with polyester fiberfill; hand sew the opening closed.

For the cording, cut three 2–yard six–ply lengths of garnet (DMC 815) and three 2–yard six-ply lengths of blue-green

Happy Holidays Pillow and House Ornament

Happy Holidays Pillow and House Ornament Key

CROSS-STITCH (2X)

ANCHOR		DMC	
231	/	453	Shell gray
683	▲	500	Blue-green
590	·	712	Cream
891	✕	729	Old gold
043	■	815	Garnet
144	◯	3325	Baby blue

ATTACHMENT

✕ 12179 Silver Heart Button –
pillow only

✕ 12179 Mill Hill Glass
Treasures tree –
ornament only

Pillow stitch count:
50 high x 59 wide

Pillow finished design size:
32-count fabric – 3 1/8 x 3 5/8 inches

Ornament stitch count:
50 high x 41 wide

Ornament finished design size:
14-count fabric – 3 1/2 x 3 inches

Teddy Bear Bib

Teddy Bear Bib

Supplies

- Purchased bib with a 1¾"-wide 16-count Aida-cloth insert
- Cotton embroidery floss
- Kreinik blending filament

Stitches

Center and stitch the chart on the Aida-cloth bib insert. Use two plies of floss to work the stitches over one square of the fabric unless otherwise specified. Press the finished bib from the back.

Teddy Bear Bib Key

CROSS-STITCH (2X)

ANCHOR		DMC	
374	◨	167	Yellow-beige
9046	✕	321	Christmas red
1046	▽	435	Chestnut
874	◫	676	Old gold
239	⊞	702	Christmas green
256	╱	704	Chartreuse
380	■	779	Cocoa
137	⊞	798	Delft blue
354	✳	840	Beige-brown
379	◯	3863	Mocha-beige

BLENDED-NEEDLE CROSS-STITCH

002	⊡	000	White (1X) and
		100	Kreinik White blending filament (1X)

BACKSTITCH (1X)

211	╱	505	Jade green – green sweater
065	╱	777	Dark raspberry – red sweater
148	╱	803	Dark baby blue – blue sweater
382	╱	3371	Black-brown – all other stitches

FRENCH KNOT

380	●	779	Cocoa – teddy bear eyes (2X wrapped twice)
382	●	3371	Black-brown – tag on middle bear (1X wrapped twice)

Stitch count: 26 high x 86 wide
Finished design size:
16-count fabric –1⅝ x 5⅜ inches

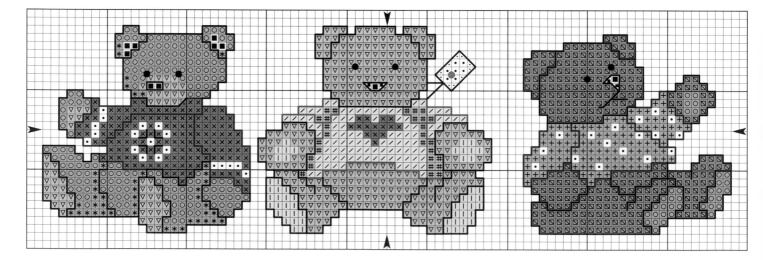

TIP: Working with Beads

When working with beads, it is important to get the bead to sit on its edge so the hole is not showing. There are two methods that work well to get this effect. The first is to stitch the bead with a half cross-stitch, using two plies of floss. Then come up to finish the cross-stitch and split the floss over the bead, pulling tightly.

The second method works better on softer fabrics (such as Cashel linen). Use one-ply floss and begin a cross-stitch. String the bead and complete the half cross-stitch. As you complete the cross-stitch, go through the hole again, pulling tightly.

Santa in Chimney Jar Topper

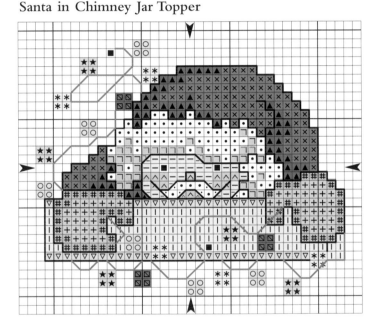

Santa in Chimney Jar Topper Key

CROSS-STITCH (2X)

ANCHOR		DMC
002	•	000 White
403	■	310 Black
9046	✕	321 Christmas red
9575	◣	353 Dark peach
210	▦	562 Medium seafoam
208	✚	563 True seafoam
1005	▲	816 Garnet
921	▽	932 True antique blue
1012	—	948 Light peach
040	⊐	3023 Brown-gray
1031	∥	3753 Pale antique blue

BACKSTITCH (1X)

	╱	025 Kreinik gray #4 very fine braid – lights wire
403	╱	310 Black – all other stitches

MILL HILL SEED BEAD

ANCHOR		DMC
290	✳	307 Lemon and 2059 Crayon yellow seed bead
257	⊙	703 Chartreuse and 2066 Crayon yellow-green seed bead
035	◩	892 Carnation and 2062 Crayon light crimson seed bead
1089	★	3845 Bright turquoise and 2064 Crayon sky blue seed bead

Santa No. 1 stitch count:
29 high x 35 wide

Santa No. 1 finished design size:
18-count fabric – 1⅝ x 1⅞ inches

Santa in Chimney Jar Topper

Supplies
- 8" square of 18-count white Aida cloth
- Cotton embroidery floss
- Kreinik very fine braid
- Mill Hill seed beads
- Jelly jar with jar ring and lid
- Lightweight fleece
- Erasable fabric marker

Stitches
Center and stitch the desired chart on the Aida cloth. Use two plies of floss to work the stitches over one square of the fabric unless otherwise specified. Attach the seed beads with two plies of matching floss. Press the stitched piece from the back.

Assembly
Center the jar lid on the back of the stitched piece. Use the erasable fabric marker to trace around the jar lid onto the stitched piece. Cut out ½" beyond the marked line. Trace the jar lid onto the fleece; cut out the fleece circle along the traced line.

Center the fleece on the front of the lid. Hand-sew running stitches ¼" from the edges of the stitched piece. Center the stitched piece face up on the fleece. Pull the thread ends to pull the edges of the stitched piece to the back of the lid; knot the thread ends to secure. Place the lid on the jar and screw on the jar ring.

Santa Jar Toppers

Hands-Up Santa Jar Topper

Supplies
- 8" square of 18-count white Aida cloth
- Cotton embroidery floss
- Kreinik very fine braid
- Mill Hill seed beads
- Jelly jar with jar ring and lid
- Lightweight fleece
- Erasable fabric marker

Stitches
Center and stitch the desired chart on the Aida cloth. Use two plies of floss to work the stitches over one square of the fabric unless otherwise specified. Attach the seed beads with one ply of matching floss. Press the stitched piece from the back.

Assembly
Center the jar lid on the back of the stitched piece. Use the erasable fabric marker to trace around the jar lid onto the stitched piece. Cut out ½" beyond the marked line. Trace the jar lid onto the fleece; cut out the fleece circle along the traced line.

Center the fleece on the front of the lid. Hand-sew running stitches ¼" from the edges of the stitched piece. Center the stitched piece face-up on the fleece. Pull the thread ends to pull the edges of the stitched piece to the back of the lid; knot the thread ends to secure. Place the lid on the jar and screw on the jar ring.

Hands-Up Santa Jar Topper Key

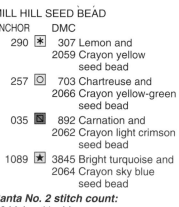

CROSS-STITCH (2X)

ANCHOR		DMC	
002	⋅	000	White
403	■	310	Black
9046	✕	321	Christmas red
9575	∧	353	Dark peach
210	#	562	Medium seafoam
208	+	563	True seafoam
1005	▲	816	Garnet
1012	−	948	Light peach
040	⌐	3023	Brown-gray

BACKSTITCH (1X)

	╱	025	Kreinik gray #4 very fine braid – lights wire
403	╱	310	Black – all other stitches

MILL HILL SEED BEAD

ANCHOR		DMC	
290	✳	307	Lemon and 2059 Crayon yellow seed bead
257	◯	703	Chartreuse and 2066 Crayon yellow-green seed bead
035	◪	892	Carnation and 2062 Crayon light crimson seed bead
1089	★	3845	Bright turquoise and 2064 Crayon sky blue seed bead

Santa No. 2 stitch count:
40 high x 41 wide

Santa No. 2 finished design size:
18-count fabric – 2¼ x 2¼ inches

Hands-Up Santa Jar Topper

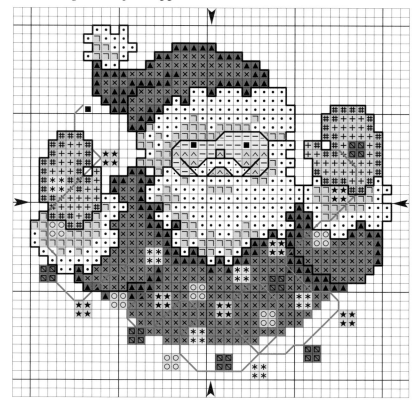

Noah's Ark Jewelry Charm

Supplies
- 5" square of 40-count silk gauze
- Cotton embroidery floss
- Medium-weight cardboard
- 1⅝×1" jewelry charm frame
- Felt scrap
- Thick white crafts glue
- ⅛"-wide ribbon

Stitches
Center and stitch chart on evenweave fabric using basket-weave stitches. Use one ply of floss to work stitches over one thread of fabric. Trim ½ inch beyond stitching.

Assembly
Cut out cardboard to fit inside of charm frame. Center stitchery over cardboard and glue in place, folding fabric edges to back. Let dry. Insert into frame. Cut felt to cover back of stitchery; glue. Tie a ribbon bow through hanger loop.

Noah's Ark Jewelry Charm

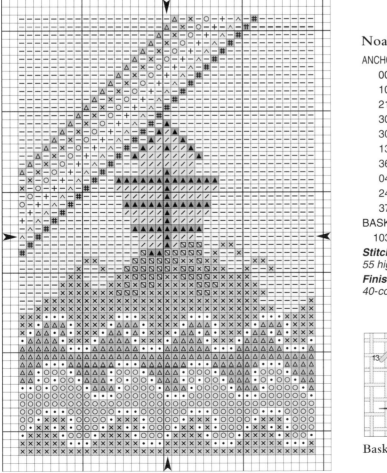

Noah's Ark Jewelry Charm Key

ANCHOR		DMC	
002	•	000	White
108	△	210	Lavender
214	○	368	Pistachio
303	∧	742	Tangerine
301	+	744	Yellow
130	×	809	Delft blue
360	▲	839	Beige-brown
042	#	961	Rose-pink
243	◨	988	Forest green
373	⁄	3828	Hazel
BASKET-WEAVE STITCH (1X)			
1031	–	3753	Antique blue

Stitch count:
55 high x 37 wide

Finished design size:
40-count fabric – 1³/₈ x 1 inches

Basket-Weave Stitches

Starry Night and Heart Jewelry Charms

Starry Night Jewelry Charm

Supplies
- 5" square of 40-count silk gauze
- Cotton embroidery floss
- Rayon embroidery floss
- Medium-weight cardboard
- ¾×1" jewelry charm frame
- Felt scrap
- Thick white crafts glue
- ⅛"-wide ribbon

Stitches
Center and stitch chart on evenweave fabric using basket weave stitches as shown in the diagram, *page 115*. Use one ply of floss to work stitches over one thread of fabric. Trim ½ inch beyond stitching.

Assembly
Cut out cardboard to fit inside of charm frame. Center stitchery over cardboard and glue in place, folding fabric edges to back. Let dry. Insert into frame. Cut felt to cover back of stitchery; glue. Tie a ribbon bow through hanger loop.

TIP: Working on Very Fine Fabric

When working on a very fine fabric (such as 40-count silk gauze), use a magnifying glass to help you see. There are many types of magnifying glasses on the market: headbands, ones that mount on your stitching frame, ones that hang around your neck, and ones that attach to a lamp.

Starry Night Jewelry Charm

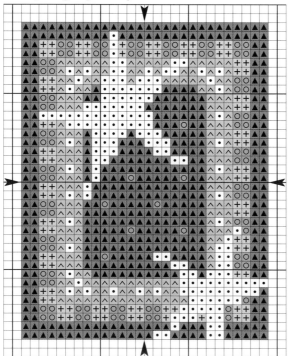

Starry Night Jewelry Charm Key

HALF CROSS-STITCH (1X)

ANCHOR		DMC	
002	⊡	35200	White rayon floss
108	⋀	210	Lavender
118	⊙	340	Medium periwinkle
117	⊞	341	Light periwinkle

BASKET-WEAVE STITCH (1X)

119	▲	333	Deep periwinkle

Stitch count:
36 high x 28 wide

Finished design size:
40-count fabric – 1 x ¾ inch

Heart Jewelry Charm

Supplies
- 5" square of 40-count silk gauze
- Cotton embroidery floss
- Medium-weight cardboard
- ⅞×1⅛" jewelry charm frame
- Felt scrap
- Thick white crafts glue
- ¼"-wide ribbon

Stitches
Center and stitch chart on evenweave fabric using basket weave stitches as shown in the diagram, *page 115*. Use one ply of floss to work stitches over one thread of fabric. Trim ½ inch beyond stitching.

Assembly
Cut out cardboard to fit inside of charm frame. Center stitchery over cardboard and glue in place, folding fabric edges to back. Let dry. Insert into frame. Cut felt to cover back of stitchery; glue. Tie a ribbon bow through hanger loop.

TIP: Types of Magnifiers

Here are some types of magnifiers you can find on the market. The headband type drops a magni-shield in front of your eyes for a larger view. The type that mounts to your stitching frame has a flexible arm so you can adjust it to your needs. The type that hangs around your neck can be balanced across your chest. A magnifying lens that attaches to a lamp can be moved for greater or less magnification. Many stitchers find that this type is more stable and easier to keep focused on the area being stitched.

Heart Jewelry Charm

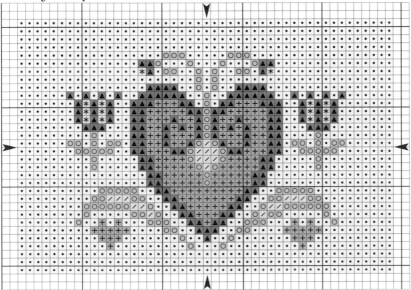

Heart Jewelry Charm Key

HALF CROSS-STITCH (1X)

ANCHOR		DMC	RAINBOW GALLERY
059	▲	326	S822 Red
119	+	333	S808 Purple
923	○	699	S829 Christmas green
307	*	783	S909 Goldenrod
205	╱	912	S828 Light Christmas green

BASKET-WEAVE STITCH (1X)

1035	•	930	S916 Dark antique blue

Stitch count:
32 high x 47 wide

Finished design size:
40-count fabric – ⅞ x 1⅛ inches

Jolly Old Elf

Jolly Old Elf Key

CROSS-STITCH (2X)

Anchor		DMC	
926	·		Ecru
897	⊠	221	Deep shell pink
1027	○	223	Medium shell pink
403	■	310	Black
374	✳	420	Medium hazel
683	▲	500	Deep blue-green
878	◉	501	Dark blue-green
391	╱	644	Light beige-gray
360	⌗	839	Beige-brown
851	＋	924	Gray-blue
1010	−	951	Ivory
373	⊥	3828	True hazel

BACKSTITCH

926	╱		Ecru – eyebrows (4X)
403	╱	310	Black – nose (1X), coat detail (2X)
391	╱	644	Light beige-gray – coat detail (2X)
360	╱	839	Dark beige-gray – beard and moustache (1X)

STRAIGHT STITCH (2X)

403	╱	310	Black – coat detail

DOUBLE LEVIATHAN STITCH (2X)

403	✳	310	Black – button

Stitch count: *126 high x 76 wide*
Finished design size:
32-count fabric – 7⁷/₈ x 4³/₄ inches

Jolly Old Elf

Supplies

- 14×18-piece of 32-count antique ivory Belfast linen
- Cotton embroidery floss
- Desired frame

Stitches

Center and stitch the design on the fabric. Use two plies of floss to work the stitches over two threads of the fabric. Press the finished stitchery carefully from the back. Frame piece as desired.

Tip: Exploring Options

Try changing the colors of a design for a whole new look. Instead of the subdued country look of this piece, you could opt for a more traditional flair with bright reds and greens instead of the muted greens, beige-brown, and beige-grays. And instead of framing the piece, finish it as a small bellpull or turn it into a decorative pillow.

Double Leviathan Stitch

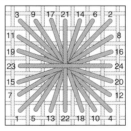

Gingerbread Man Tray

Gingerbread Man Tray

Supplies
- 18×22" piece of 14-count white Aida cloth
- Cotton embroidery floss
- 10×13" piece of fleece
- Needle; embroidery hoop
- Purchased 10×13" wood tea tray with a 7¾×10¾" design area
- Spray adhesive
- Thick white crafts glue or tape

Stitches
Center and stitch the chart on the fabric. Use three plies of floss to work the cross-stitches. Work the blended-needle stitches as specified in the key. Use one ply of floss to work the backstitches. Work the French knots using one ply of floss wrapped once around the needle. Press the finished stitchery carefully from the back.

Assembly
Cut the fleece the same size as the mounting board from the tray. Spray the board lightly with the adhesive and position the fleece on top. Center the wrong side of the stitchery over the fleece on the board; tape or glue the edges to the back. Insert the design into the tray; reassemble the tray following the manufacturer's instructions.

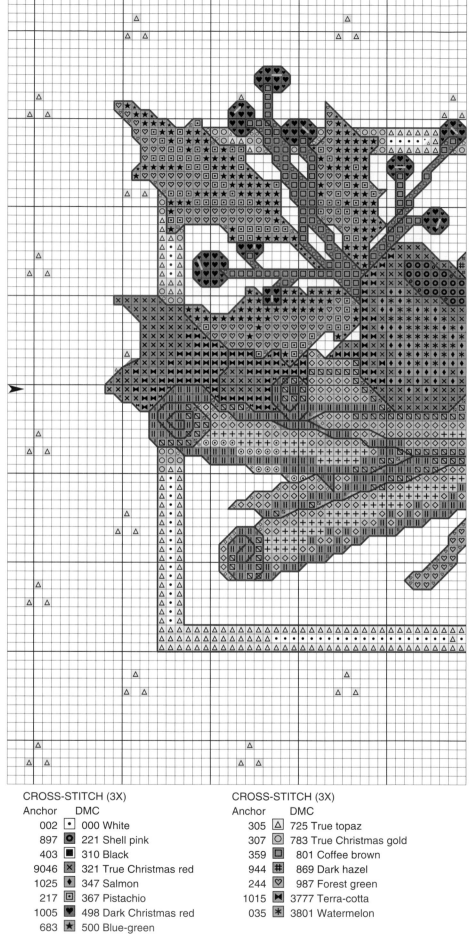

CROSS-STITCH (3X)			CROSS-STITCH (3X)		
Anchor	DMC		Anchor	DMC	
002	·	000 White	305	△	725 True topaz
897	◉	221 Shell pink	307	○	783 True Christmas gold
403	■	310 Black	359	▦	801 Coffee brown
9046	✕	321 True Christmas red	944	#	869 Dark hazel
1025	◆	347 Salmon	244	♡	987 Forest green
217	▫	367 Pistachio	1015	◤	3777 Terra-cotta
1005	♥	498 Dark Christmas red	035	✻	3801 Watermelon
683	★	500 Blue-green			

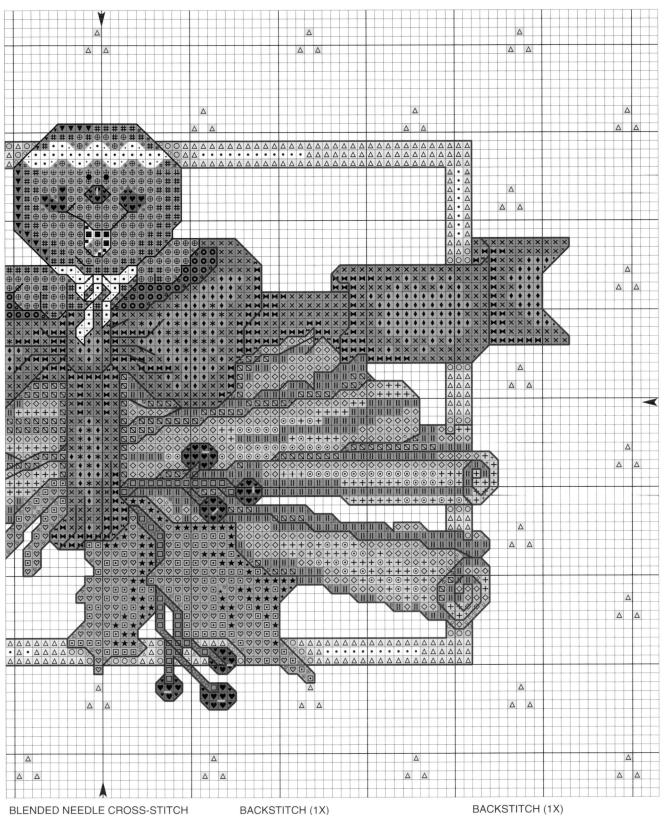

BLENDED NEEDLE CROSS-STITCH

Anchor   DMC

BLENDED NEEDLE CROSS-STITCH

374	⊕	420 Medium hazel (1X) and
308		782 Medium topaz (2X)
374	‖	420 Medium hazel (1X) and
944		869 Dark hazel (2X)
374	▣	420 Medium hazel (2X) and
944		869 Dark hazel (1X)
1045	◇	436 Dark tan (2X) and
308		782 Medium topaz (1X)

BACKSTITCH (1X)

Anchor   DMC

1045	⊞	436 Dark tan (2X) and
1002		977 Light golden brown (1X)
362	⊙	437 Medium tan (2X) and
363		3827 Pale golden brown (1X)
944	▼	869 Dark hazel (2X) and
360		3031 Mocha (1X)
403	╱	310 Black – gingerbread man, mouth, and bow tie
236	╱	3799 Charcoal – all other stitches

BACKSTITCH (1X)

Anchor   DMC

STRAIGHT STITCH (1X)

002	╱	000 White – berry and nose highlights

FRENCH KNOT (1X wrapped once)

403	●	310 Black – eyes

Stitch count: *85 high x 122 wide*

Finished design size:
14-count fabric – 6 x 8⅝ inches

Cross-Stitch Basics

Getting Started

The written instructions for each project indicate where to begin stitching. For most projects the starting point is at the center. Every chart has arrows that indicate the horizontal and vertical centers. With your finger, trace along the grid to the point where the two centers meet. Compare a symbol at the center of the chart to the key and choose which floss color to stitch first. To find the center of the fabric, fold it into quarters and finger-crease or baste along the folds with a single ply of contrasting floss.

Cut the floss into 15" lengths, and separate all six plies. Recombine the plies as indicated in the project instructions, and thread them into a blunt-tip needle.

Basic Cross-Stitch

Make one cross-stitch for each symbol on the chart. For horizontal rows, stitch the first diagonal of each stitch in the row. Work back across the row, completing each stitch. On most linen and even-weave fabrics, work the stitches over two threads as shown in the diagram *below*. For Aida cloth, each stitch fills one square.

You also can work cross-stitches in the reverse direction. Remember to

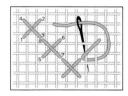

Cross-stitch worked singly

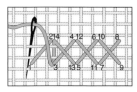

Cross-stitch worked in rows

embroider the stitches uniformly—that is, always work the top half of each stitch in the same direction.

To secure thread at the beginning

The most common way to secure the beginning tail of the thread is to hold it under the first four or five stitches.

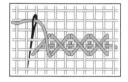

Stitching over the thread tail

To secure the thread with a waste knot, thread the needle and knot the end of the thread. Insert the needle from the right side of fabric, about 4 inches away from the first stitch. Bring the needle up through the fabric, and work the first series of stitches. When finished, clip the knot on the right side. Rethread the needle with excess floss and push the needle through to the stitches on the wrong side of the fabric.

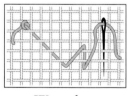

Waste knot

When working with two, four, or six plies of floss, use a loop knot. Cut half as many plies of thread, making each one twice as long. Recombine the plies, fold the strand in half, and thread all of the ends into the needle. Work the first

Loop knot

diagonal of the first stitch, and slip the needle through the loop formed by folding the thread.

To secure thread at the end

To finish, slip the threaded needle under previously stitched threads on the wrong side of the fabric for four or five stitches, weaving the thread back and forth a few times. Clip the thread.

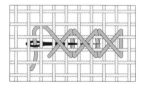

Securing thread at the end

Smyrna Cross-Stitch

A Smyrna cross-stitch consists of an X-shape stitch topped by a straight horizontal stitch and a straight vertical stitch. It's often worked over four, six, eight, or more threads.

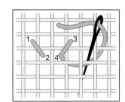

Smyrna cross-stitch

Quarter and Three-Quarter Cross-Stitches

To obtain rounded shapes in a design, use quarter and three-quarter cross-stitches. On linen and even-weave fabrics, a quarter cross-stitch will extend from the corner to the center intersection of the threads. To make quarter cross-stitches on Aida cloth, estimate the

Quarter stitches

center of the square. Three-quarter cross-stitches combine a quarter cross-stitch with a half cross-stitch. Both stitches may slant in any direction.

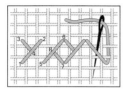

Three-quarter stitches

Backstitches

Backstitches define and outline the shapes of a design. For most projects, backstitches require only one ply of floss. On the color key, (2X) indicates two plies of floss, (3X) indicates three plies, etc.

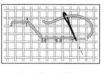

Backstitches

Couching

Use two needles to work a line of couching. Bring the heavier couched thread through the fabric at the beginning of the line designated on the chart and to the back at the end. Roughly align it in the position indicated on the chart. Bring the lighter couching thread through the fabric four threads (unless otherwise specified on chart) beyond the entry point of the couched thread, over it, and to the back in the next hole. Move four threads along the line of the couched thread, and repeat the couching. Continue along

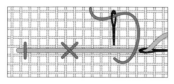

Couching

the entire length of the couched thread.

Algerian Eyelet

The key to making this spoked stitch with its center hole is to work from the outside in. Bring the needle from the back to the front at an outside edge of the stitch, then push it to the back at the midpoint of the stitch, pulling the thread firmly and gently. As you work successive spokes, an opening will appear in the middle.

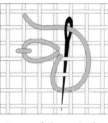

Algerian eyelets in a row

Chain Stitch

Bring the needle to the front of the fabric, and return to the back through the same hole, forming a loop. Slide the tip of the needle under two or more threads and bring it to the front of the fabric. Slip the loop under the needle tip. Pull gently until the loop lies smoothly on the fabric. Pass the needle to the back, forming the loop of the second stitch of the chain.

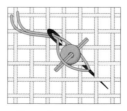

Chain stitches

Cross-Stitches with Beads

Beads may be attached by working the first half of each cross-stitch and attaching a bead on the return stitch. To ensure that beads stand up straight,

Securing a bead

work with two plies of floss and add the bead to the first half stitch. As you work the second diagonal, split the plies so one ply lies on each side of the bead.

Lazy-Daisy Stitch

Bring the needle to the front of the fabric, and return to the back through the same hole, forming a loop. Slide the tip of the needle under two or more threads; then bring it to the front of the fabric. Slip the loop under the needle tip. Pull gently until the loop lies smoothly on the fabric. Push the needle to the back, forming a tack stitch over the end of the loop.

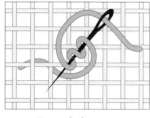

Lazy daisy stitch

French Knot

Bring the threaded needle through the fabric, and wrap the floss around the needle as shown. Tighten the twists, and return the needle through the fabric in the same place. The floss will slide through the wrapped thread to make the knot.

French knot

Half Cross-Stitches

A half cross-stitch is a single diagonal or half a cross-stitch. They usually are listed under a separate heading in the color

Cross-Stitch Basics

key and are indicated on the chart by a diagonal colored line.

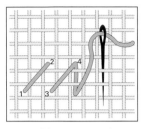

Half cross-stitch

Running Stitch

Running stitches work up fast and add design definition. They are usually equal in length, although uneven stitches create a novelty effect.

Running stitches

Straight Stitches

The simplest of all stitches, straight stitches often are used for sun rays, whiskers, and other simple accents.

Straight stitches

Satin Stitch

This smooth-surface stitch may be worked over a few or many threads. Bring up the needle up through the first hole. Count threads along a straight line, and return to the back of the fabric. For the second stitch, bring up the needle

Satin stitches

through the hole immediately next to the first stitch.

Changing Materials

Many stitchers work cross-stitch designs using fabrics and threads other than those specified in the projects. Use this helpful information to complete the projects in this book while adapting them to your own preferences.

Before you begin a project on a fabric other than that specified, stitch a small sample. Be sure you're happy with the amount of detail on the new fabric and the way the thread covers it. Also note whether the needle slips smoothly through the fabric.

Cross-Stitch Fabrics

Work counted cross-stitch on any fabric that lets you make consistently sized, even stitches. Many fabrics marketed specifically for cross-stitch are interchangeable when the stitch-per-inch counts match. For example, a project that calls for 28-count linen stitched over two threads can easily be worked on 14-count Aida. A higher count fabric will yield a smaller project. When a design is enlarged by working on lower count fabric, some of the detail may be lost. The charts in this book indicate the size of the design when worked on the recommended fabric.

Aida cloth is the most popular cross-stitch fabric. The threads are woven in groups separated by tiny spaces to create a pattern of squares across the surface of the fabric so a beginning stitcher can easily see where to place the cross-stitches. Measure Aida cloth by the number of squares per inch; for example, 14-count Aida cloth has 14 squares per inch. Look for Aida cloth in 6, 8, 11, 14, 16, and 18 thread counts. You'll find 14-count Aida cloth in more than 60 colors. For beginners, white Aida cloth is available with a removable grid of pre-basted threads.

Experienced stitchers consider linen

the standard of excellence in cross-stitch fabrics. The threads used to weave linen vary in thickness, giving the fabric a slightly irregular surface. Measure thread count by the number of threads per inch. Because most designs are worked over two threads, 28-count linen usually yields 14 stitches per inch. Linens are made in counts from 14 (seven stitches per inch) to 45.

The market for specialty fabrics for counted cross-stitch continues to grow with the popularity of the craft. These fabrics are referred to as even-weave fabrics because they're woven from threads with a consistent diameter, although some have a homespun look. Count most even-weaves like linen—by the number of threads per inch—and stitch over two threads.

Use Hardanger fabric for very fine counted cross-stitch. The traditional fabric for Norwegian embroidery of the same name has an over-two, under-two weave that produces 22 small squares per inch.

Use waste canvas to cross-stitch on clothing and fabrics that aren't otherwise suitable for stitching. The canvas marks the squares and is designed to ravel when dampened after stitching is complete. It ranges in count from 6½ to 20 stitches per inch.

Cross-stitch charts can be worked 32- or 40-count silk gauze, 14-count perforated paper, 6- to 24-count needlepoint canvas, or plastic canvas. These materials make no provision for fractional (quarter and three-quarter) stitches, so choose a chart with whole stitches only.

Threads for Stitching

Most types of commercially available embroidery thread are adaptable for counted cross-stitch projects.

Six-ply cotton embroidery floss has the widest range of colors, including variegated colors. It separates easily into single or multiple plies for stitching. The instructions with each project in this book list how many plies to use. If you select a different-count fabric than the one specified, use the chart on *page 16* as a guide, and experiment on a scrap of the fabric until you achieve the desired effect. A greater number of plies will result in a dense or heavily textured piece; a smaller number of plies will create a lightweight or delicate texture.

Rayon and silk floss are similar in weight to six-ply cotton embroidery floss but with a higher sheen. Both can be interchanged with cotton floss, one ply for one ply. Because they have a "slicker" texture, you may find them more difficult to use.

Pearl cotton is available in four sizes: #3, #5, #8, and #12 (#3 is heavy; #12 is fine). It has an obvious twist and a high sheen.

Flower thread is a matte-finish cotton thread that is no longer available in the United States. When a design calls for flower thread, substitute two plies of floss for one strand of flower thread.

A product growing in popularity is overdyed thread. Most colors have an irregularly variegated, one-of-a-kind appearance. Cotton floss, silk floss, flower thread, and pearl cotton are all available in this form. All produce a soft, shaded appearance without changing thread colors. The color changes can be enhanced by working each stitch individually.

Specialty threads add a distinctive look to cross-stitch work. They range in weight from hair-fine blending filament, usually used with floss, to ⅛-inch-wide ribbon. Specialty threads include numerous metallic threads, richly colored and textured threads, and fun-to-stitch glow-in-the-dark threads.

Needle Types

Blunt-tip needles work best on most cross-stitch fabrics because they slide through the holes and between threads without splitting or snagging the fibers.

A large-eyed needle accommodates most threads. Some companies sell such needles labeled "cross-stitch," but they're identical to tapestry needles—blunt tipped and large eyed. Use the chart on *page 16* to guide you to the right needle size for common fabrics.

An exception to the blunt-tip needle is waste canvas. Since it's usually basted to a tightly woven fabric, a sharp embroidery needle is required to penetrate the fabric beneath.

Seed beads require very fine needles that will slide through the holes. Two readily available options are a #8 quilting needle, which is short with a tiny eye, and a long beading needle, which has a longer eye.

Calculating Finished Design Sizes

At the end of each cross-stitch key you'll find a finished design size. The dimensions given are for the stitched area of that particular project on the recommended fabric. For example, the Santa design on *page 59* has a finished design size of 5¼ by 5½ inches on the key. The stitch count of the design is

73 high by 77 wide. The Santa design was stitched over one square of 14-count Aida cloth. To calculate the finished design size, divide the number of stitches high and the number wide by the fabric count. For the Santa design, the figures are as follows: $73 \div 14 = 5\frac{3}{14}$ (rounded off to 7¼) and $77 \div 14 = 5\frac{1}{2}$..

If a design is stitched on an even-weave fabric, it normally is stitched over two threads. For example, if stitching over two threads on 28-count fabric, you would divide the stitch count by 14 instead of 28.

Knowing how to calculate finished design sizes opens up stitching options, allowing you to choose other fabrics than what a project recommends, therefore changing the size of a finished design. The higher the stitch count of the fabric, the smaller the finished piece.

Here is a sample of size changes for a design that is 120 stitches high and 90 stitches wide:

On 14-count fabric, 8½ × 6½ inches
On 18-count fabric, 6⅔ × 5 inches
On 20-count fabric, 6 × 4½ inches

Index